WWII

"OPERATION WATCHTOWER"

No one had ever tried attacking the Japanese in their Pacific islands. They were still unbeaten, still expanding their empire.

But hard-eyed Admiral Ernest J. King, Chief of Naval Operations, knew that the time to start was now.

He didn't know that they'd hold out in the caves and dugouts to the last man, to the last hour, until they had to be burned out one by one.

He didn't know about the deadly, precision night attacks the Japanese fleet had been practising for generations.

Nobody knew about island war.

This is the story of how American sailors and marines learned their trade—at bloody Guadalcanal.

THE NAVY AT GUADALCANAL

STAN SMITH

SPECIAL INTRODUCTION BY
ADMIRAL ARLEIGH A. BURKE, USN (RET.)

LANCER BOOKS · NEW YORK

A LANCER BOOK • 1966

THE NAVY AT GUADALCANAL

Copyright © 1963 by Stan Smith

LANCER BOOKS, INC. • 185 MADISON AVENUE • NEW YORK, N.Y. 10016

ACKNOWLEDGMENTS

The author acknowledges with gratitude the following persons who did so much to make this book possible: Rear Admiral John S. McCain, Jr., USN; Mr. Dean Allard, Naval History Division; Cdr. Russell L. Bufkins, USNR; Lt. Cdr. David M. Cooney, USN; Lt. Cdr. F. H. Prehn, USN: Yeoman 2/c Anthony Metro, USN; and Miss Mollie Thompson of the Australian Consular Library. A salute also to the many persons who were kind enough to recall individual accounts of the fighting.

Stan Smith
New York, N.Y.

──────── **ABOUT THE AUTHOR** ────────

Stan Smith served in the Atlantic on the USS Arkansas and in the Pacific on the submarine Lionfish during World War II. He is a member of the Navy League, Sub Vets of World War II, and an associate of the United States Naval Institute. He has written a daily column for the New York News and television documentaries for NBC, in addition to having written for movies and magazines.

Dedicated to the memory of Admirals Lee, Callaghan and Scott, and to the officers and bluejackets who fell at Guadalcanal.

CONTENTS

			PAGE
PROLOGUE			11
PART I	Savo Island		15
PART II	Eastern Solomons		52
	Parry and Thrust		65
PART III	Cape Esperance		78
	Guadalcanal Blues		93
PART IV	Santa Cruz Islands		100
PART V	Guadalcanal		112
PART VI	Tassafaronga		142
PART VII	Guadalcanal Secured		154
BIBLIOGRAPHY			158

FOREWORD

The battles so vividly described in the following pages will bring back equally vivid memories to those who participated in them—and lived. Many mistakes were made in these battles by both sides—mistakes made by men dead tired—by men who fought night after night—day after day, by men who had to make crucial decisions on very little information of what the capabilities of the enemy were and what the enemy might do.

Mr. Smith's book highlights very effectively the relatively small—sometimes of hairbreadth dimensions—difference between victory and defeat. And this difference is the margin between men who become great and those who miss greatness.

If Admiral Mikawa had not retired after his stunning victory at Savo Island, he might very well have altered the entire course of the war in the Pacific. As a matter of fact, if there was one ingredient the hard fighting Japanese lacked in their personal makeup it was this intangible flicker of will to go the extra step. Certainly they were men of indomitable courage and they discovered quite early the advantages of skilled teamwork. They were expert ship handlers as they had already demonstrated to the Russian Navy some years before. The night actions off Guadalcanal are also eloquent testimony to their seamanship.

But the Japanese were hampered by individual uncertainty. They did not develop the self-confidence which makes a man put his trust in his own judgment at a critical period regardless of what the "book" may recommend. And it was this failing that contributed to the loss of effectiveness of the Imperial Japanese Navy.

While there is no doubt that United States Forces would have in time overcome the Japanese through sheer weight of power, the war would have been prolonged perhaps much longer if the senior officers of the IJN particularly had had the willingness to make that one extra thrust where there was no guide but their own judgment. We can be thankful that that characteristic has been a part of our national character since the days of the American Revolution. It was never demonstrated more effectively than in the battles of the Pacific.

There are also some material deficiencies Mr. Smith points out which remain critical today. Perhaps they will always be critical.

Of primary importance is the necessity for a reliable and instantaneous communication system. In the various phases of the engagements discussed in this book, the failure or lack of such communications is apparent.

Another item is the thoroughness of training together. This is just as important today as it was in the days of World War II. The knowledge of how another man thinks, how he reacts and an understanding of his character, can mean the difference between winning or losing a battle.

We learned this lesson well and we are still striving to perfect the system in such a way that ships of not only our own Navy, but those from Navies with which we operate in concert know what to expect in joint maneuvers.

Mr. Smith has taken just one chapter from the greatest conflict yet experienced by man. In this book he has reflected with great insight, the courage, the integrity and the will and, in some cases, the failure, of men at war.

Arleigh Burke

PROLOGUE

THE SOLOMON ISLANDS, discovered by Spanish explorer Don Alvarado Medana in 1568, were re-discovered by the American GI in 1942-43. Situated a few derees below the Equator, west of the sub-continent of New Georgia, Guadalcanal became a synonym for disease and death when stories of a distant emerald hell hit front pages shortly after the United States invasion in August 1942. New Georgia Sound, aptly nicknamed The Slot by American sailors, flows on a northeast-southwest track for the entire length of the chain, or for about 600 miles. The islands—Bougainville, Shortland, Malaita, Choiseul, New Georgia, Florida, Tulagi, Guadalcanal, Russells, Santa Isabel, San Cristobal—monopolized headlines as the scene of bloody, internecine conflict between the United States and Japan.

There were, and still are, a number of Americans who hold that the recapture of the Solomons was hardly worth the prohibitive expenditure in men and ships. Military people, conversely, believe that invasion was necessary at this time in order to catch the enemy offguard following his defeat at Midway. Notwithstanding these strong arguments, the fact remains that in addition to the bitter campaigns of the Army and Marines, the Navy, operating under the aegis of the United States lost an aggregate of 126,000 tons of warships and thousands of seamen in the process of conducting six major engagements in these waters. Even with a perspective of twenty years the names of Savo, "Tokyo Express," "Watchtower," still retain a vivid and trenchant clarity for all concerned.

Until the arrival of Task Forces 61 and 62, here stood

the Australian coastwatcher. Alone but for his Melanesian natives, he risked instant death spying on Japanese movements in the islands. Cranking up his portable tele-radio, the coastwatcher would pass along word of enemy movements to his headquarters in Sydney, Australia, via an inter-island network which the Japanese were unable to silence at any time during the campaign. Search the records of the war in the Pacific and you will not find a braver, more dedicated coterie of men than these few; nor their porters and native troops.

With a long history of flesh eating and headhunting, the Melanesian made an admirable adjustment to the presence of the white man. When Tulagi was chosen as the site of a Royal Navy coaling station at the turn of the century, the Melanesians, short of stature, woolly-headed, tough (a Navy Cross, for example, went to Sergeant Vouza of the Tulagi constabulary) fought and, in many instances, died with the coastwatcher.

Guadalcanal and Tulagi, at the southern end of the Solomons group, were primary targets of the invasion. Of the former, no man had a kind word: Guadalcanal was muddy and malaria-infested, and it rained more often than not, particularly in the winter; forbidding mountain ranges rose 8,000 feet above the floor of its sweltering jungle. In the lowlands, there were vast fields of kunai grass which stretched out for miles. A few prospectors lived in the ridges and scratched the alluvial sands for grains of gold, while below there were copra planters who apparently made a go of it in this grim and solitary confinement. But that was all. Nobody actually came to the island unless he *had* to, and even then his stay was indeed brief.

Tulagi, by contrast, was almost pleasant. A community of British rule, with an Australian Air Force base, still more copra plantations, a town of sorts where a man could cheerfully and comfortably remain drunk for weeks, a Lever Brothers trading post and even tennis courts, Tulagi was the seat of civilized living in the islands. The shopkeepers were Chinese, descendants of the 400 who had swum across when the schooner *St. Paul* fought it out with King Solomon's shoals in 1865, and lost the argument. Civilization made no real impression on these islands, however, and, until the invasion that hurled them into world limelight they remained an illusory and inhospitable blot on the emerald face of the South Pacific.

On April 17, 1942, the day after his arrival from London where he had served the past two years as Special Naval Observer, Vice Admiral Robert L. Ghormley reported to the office of Admiral Ernest J. King, the Chief of Naval Operations, for orders. The latter had been urging the President and Joint Chiefs that it was nearing the hour to take the offensive-defensive in the Pacific, for a number of reasons, including the protection of the "communications lifeline to the Anzac nations."

King presented a blueprint for Operation Watchtower and made it abundantly clear that Ghormley's new task was "both important and difficult," since there were insufficient resources for it to be carried out as desired. The vice admiral, King said, was to assemble a staff, establish headquarters in Aukland, New Zealand, and an advance base in the Fiji Islands, and be prepared to mount an amphibious invasion sometime in the autumn. It was a tall order, but one to which energetic, capable Ghormley was equal, and he immediately acted upon Admiral King's orders.

Meanwhile, Japan was moving again in the Pacific. In May, coming down from Buka, with an eye on an invasion of Port Moresby, her forces occupied Rabaul, New Britain, so that her bombers now could strike anywhere in the Solomons. However, as a result of the battle in the Coral Sea, Japan's Port Moresby invasion was derailed although Tulagi, after continuous bombing raids, was

13

occupied by a small naval force whose duties were chiefly the construction of airfields on Guadalcanal.

In June the tide turned for the United States. Navy fighters and bombers caught the Japanese invasion force converging on Midway—and routed it decisively—four first-line carriers sunk and the cream of her naval aviation shot down. Admiral King's immediate desire was to catch the enemy while he was still reeling from the effects of this battle. At a meeting of the Joint Staffs, he advanced the Solomons operation then grooming in New Zealand. Vice Admiral Ghormley, whose staff included about 50 officers, had as top men Rear Admiral Daniel J. Callaghan and Marine Brigadier Dewitt Peck. The Marines to be used in the amphibious attack were 20,000 men of the 1st Division, Major General Alexander J. Vandergrift commanding.

Tactical command of the Watchtower forces was given over to the popular veteran Vice Admiral Frank Jack Fletcher who, during the invasion, would fly his three-starred flag aboard *Saratoga*; Rear Admiral Richmond K. Turner, a tough, battle-browed spokesman for the "alligators," assumed command of the amphibious forces; Rear Admiral Victor A. C. Crutchley, RN, of Australia, was chosen to head up the support group, while all shore-based aircraft fell to capable, leathery Rear Admiral John S. McCain.

Operation Watchtower, hampered by short supplies and shorter time, moved into high gear. On July 25, and only after an American reconnaissance plane had reported an airfield on Guadalcanal, was the final irrevocable step taken: Ghormley received Admiral Chester W. Nimitz' operation order for the seizure of the Solomons.

The first expeditionary force since 1898 and the first offensive operation of the Pacific was under way.

PART I

Savo Island

THE NAVY came out of the Koro Sea and steamed in two task forces across the calm South Pacific for ten days. The weather was clear and warm, and the temperature was in the upper 70's. There were 93 warships and their train, including 23 transports which were lifting the men of the 1st Marine Division.

It was Friday, August 7, 1942.

At 2 A.M. there was a turn-to and grimly silent Marines wandered into chow to pick at their food. Usually they were garrulous men, quick to joke, quicker to rib one another. But this morning they weren't. Many of them didn't bother to enter the messhalls, but instead wandered topsides to watch the black, cloudless morning of the South Pacific.

Lining the railings, Marines listened to the gentle throbbing of diesels and the sibilant hiss of the falling bow wave—the only sounds above a terse whisper; they were almost there. Quickly now an island would rise up black and shapeless and sprawling across the entire vapid face of the sea, and that would be it. So they watched hard "like a man looking into an open grave."

An hour later, Guadalcanal came out of the sea, and then Savo Island. Now the transports and their screening ships divided into two groups—X-Ray Force (*Fuller, American Legion, Bellatrix,* flagship *McCawley, Barnett, Elliot, Libra, Hunter Liggett, President Adams* and

Ahena) steaming parallel to Guadalcanal behind heavy cruiser *Chicago*; Yoke Force (*Neville, President Jackson, Calhoun, Zeilin, Heywood, Gregory, Little*, and *Mc-Kean*) edging northward of Savo. In two columns of 15 and 8 ships they moved, and around them glided their destroyers and cruisers with all guns manned and ready.

"We will recapture Guadalcanal and Tulagi which are now in enemy hands," Rear Admiral Richmond Kelly Turner, the amphibious commander, had told them in a prepared statement read over ships' speaker systems. "In this first forward step toward clearing the Japanese out of occupied territory we have strong support from the Pacific Fleet and from the air, surface and submarine forces . . ."

There was no hostile gunfire to shatter the blackness and stitch the night with tracer trails. No tocsin sounded. The ships crept closer and the men on bridges stared over at the land mass, refusing to believe that a surprise such as this could be so complete. And yet it was—the enemy was asleep.

In the ready rooms of the three aircraft carriers, pilots listened to final briefings and all expected that the enemy would send up Zeroes to meet them. On the warships, gun captains said it was a typical Jap trick and nobody, anywhere in the task forces, was ready to admit that this well-nigh impossible approach would end in complete silence.

The hands of ships' clocks moved inexorably around to 5:30 and aboard the carrier group Vice Admiral Frank Jack Fletcher was sending off the first strike of bombers and fighters. From the dark, silent shore there *still* wasn't a sound. Transports crept into the faintly-outlined beaches in exact unloading position as planned, and the warships disported themselves off the installations to be bombarded.

Finally, at 6:13 A.M., the eight-inch guns of the heavy

16

cruiser *Quincy* spat out the first salvo of the campaign at Guadalcanal's Lunga Point and, a moment later, in a tremendous exhalation of flame and steel all warships in the two task forces joined in. A paroxysm of jagged light flashed low across the sky and on the target islands black earth, buildings, and fringing jungles heaved up in convulsive response. Soon the planes came in to bomb and strafe, and Marines—20,000 of them—standing on deck and staring at the land, saw the explosions and heard the cacophony as they waited to go ashore, and for the first time felt better.

Very quickly the planes found a target on Savo Sound, a native schooner attempting to escape, and they worked it over and set it aflame. Some thought the schooner a Jap PT-boat carrying the enemy's high command, and there were other speculations. Attention then focused on a burning oil dump and a small white building on Tulagi which had somehow remained intact throughout the first minutes of bombardment. More scuttlebutt. At 6:47 aboard the bridge of the transport *Neville*, tall, taciturn Navy Captain George B. Ashe, standing at the intercom, studied the sweep second of his watch and suddenly blurted: "Land the Landing Force!"

Higgins boats and DUKWs swung outboard on davits in preparation for the landings, at 8:05 A.M. Line of departure: 5,000 yards from the beaches.

In Tokyo, radio station JOAK was on the air with a broadcast beamed to the West Coast; an English-speaking announcer twitted his listeners: "Where are the U.S. Marines hiding? They are supposed to be the best fighters in the world, yet nobody has even seen them . . ."

Lieutenant Juntaro Maruyama, commanding officer of the Special Detachment of Kure Marines on Tulagi, was spending his last living hours in the small white building

17

which was Radio Tulagi before shells from the light cruiser *San Juan* demolished it. His death followed a nightmare of comparatively short duration.

When told of strange ships in the harbor, Maruyama had jumped out of bed and hurried up the radio tower to an observation platform. But midway along in his climb, the lieutenant saw the dark silhouettes of many ships and realized what they were. Instantly, he turned around.

In Maruyama's command were 250 Marines, crack fighters who could be depended upon to die hard; there were also 1,500 labor troops on the island, who might not die quite so hard, but who could be counted upon to put up something of a fight before surrender. These men—all of them—were ordered to fall back on pre-determined positions before the first wave of U.S. Marines stormed ashore. Maruyama sent off a contact report to Outer South Seas Force at Rabaul, 570 miles to the north. At 6:30 A.M., when the barrage was at its height, he sent an amplifying report:

"Tulagi under severe bombardment from air and sea. Enemy task force sighted. One battleship, two cruisers, three carriers, fifteen destroyers, and thirty to forty transports."

Then Juntaro Maruyama, realizing death was imminent, made his peace. A fraction of a minute later, shells from cruiser *San Juan* screamed in to obliterate the radio shack and all within it.

In Rabaul, Rear Admiral Gunichi Mikawa, commander in chief of the Eighth Fleet and Outer South Seas Force, was the recipient of the thunderbolts from Tulagi. Asleep in his headquarters building near the harbor, Mikawa, 53, quickly dressed and ordered his staff to make plans for a counter attack.

Mikawa saw the American landings as an opportunity to avenge the Midway defeat, the first real setback Japan

18

had encountered in the war. As Admiral Nagumo's Bat-div 3, Mikawa had been present when U.S. planes had bombed four first-line carriers beneath the waves. He well remembered the route of the great task force and its inglorious return to the home islands. In the aftermath, Mikawa had been relieved of command and sent home on two weeks' leave preparatory to assuming command of a new station in the Pacific.

At Setagaya, a suburb of Tokyo, Mikawa had recieved a visit from Captain Toshikazu Ohmae, his chief of staff. The two men had discussed the past and future, and then Mikawa had sent the four-striper out to the site of the Eighth Fleet on an inspection tour. When, two weeks later, Mikawa broke his two-starred flag from the ram-shackle gray building which served as his headquarters ashore in Rabaul, he was once more a happy man. Here, at last, was an opportunity to serve. Japan's aspirations, although somewhat numbed by the effects of June 4th, still ran along at a fast clip in the South Pacific.

Soft-spoken and intense, Admiral Mikawa was highly regarded as a skilled career officer and an intellectual, a *samurai* whose distinct preference was for the traditional night attack in which the Imperial Japanese Navy ex-celled. As Mikawa hurried to the messhall where his staff was already at work, the faithful Ohmae handed him still another message from the beleaguered garrison:

"Enemy effecting simultaneous landings on Tulagi and Guadalcanal. We pray for enduring fortunes of war and will defend to the death."

It was 8:05 and Ohmae said: "Well, I guess they're gone."

Mikawa nodded. "Yes," he answered, "but we're not—let's try to avenge them quickly."

In the messhall, Mikawa's staff was poring over charts of the Solomons and arranging for immediate transfer of available forces to the islands. Already en route from

Kavieng, at the head end of New Island where Mikawa kept a large portion of his sea forces as insurance against MacArthur's bombers, were heavy cruisers *Aoba*, *Kako* and *Kinugasa* whose commanding officers had intercepted the Tulagi messages and, acting on their own, had put down the coast for a rendezvous they knew would be ordered by their scrappy admiral.

Light cruisers *Tenaru*, *Yubari*, and the old destroyer *Yunagi* were also coming down, and Mikawa's flagship heavy cruiser *Chokai*, was under way at full speed.

Mikawa, with his staff, warmed to the job of vengeance.

Three destroyers were diverted from escort duty off Buna and Submarine Squadron 7, with a total of five long-range I-boats, was ordered to concentrate in the waters off Guadalcanal; two R-boats were pulled off war patrol in the sea lanes off Australia. Then Mikawa ordered the 25th Air Flotilla (Navy) to get Zeroes and Bettys aloft for an instant strike. As to present relief, there were 100 rifles of the Sasebo Special Naval Landing Force and 310 rifles from a base reserve unit at Rabaul. Transport *Meiyo Mayu* was standing by, with supply ship *Soya* and minelayer *Tsugaru* available for immediate escort duty.

"Get them under way at once—everything helps," was Mikawa's comment.

Japan's interservice rivalry prevented the Army from contributing to Mikawa's retaliatory measures, but the admiral philosophically resigned himself to using the forces at his command rather than buck red tape at the moment. So, now, there was nothing else which could possibly be done for Guadalcanal and Tulagi, and the admiral came out of the messhall and went to his bedroom to get dressed. After breakfast, the staff returned to the business of plotting a counter-attack and the morning was without incident until 10:30 A.M., when the air raid sirens began to scream in the harbor.

Mikawa and his staff hurried outside and stood in the bright, balmy morning as a flight of 12 B-17s roared directly overhead. The American target was Vunakanau airport, a few miles away, so the naval base was unharmed.

"They," Mikawa said softly as he watched the silver-tipped bombers, "are almost beautiful. Would that they were ours."

On Guadalcanal, Marines had gone ashore in landings reminiscent of practice assaults on North Carolina's seashore. Not a shot had been fired in anger. The Japs, withdrawing into the jungles, had left behind a few bicycles and burned-out trucks near the beaches when the first wave of Marines stepped ashore at 9:10.

The 1st Division's immediate objective was Grassy Knoll, a distant unattainable position because of the rugged terrain, but then this objective was changed and the amphibious force made its way through a long field of kunai grass. Two battalions of the 5th Regiment came ashore first, followed closely by the 1st Division. Both outfits worked along the shore, the former crossing the Ilu River at a sandbar near the mouth of the river and working parallel to it. In the second wave was Richard Tregaskis who, pausing under a palm tree, heard an Australian guide remark, "I'm exhausted from the arduousness of landing under such heavy fire."

Guadalcanal, although a glut of flames along the line of enemy installations, was dead quiet during most of the morning. Its total casualty list was a Marine who'd cut his hand with a machete opening a coconut. But the story of the landings on Tulagi was slightly different: Edson's Raiders found only tough sledding, and likewise the men of the second wave a few minutes later. The Japanese seaplane base was a mass of fire and five Zeroes were sinking junkpiles. Absolutely nothing remained of the Australian air force installation, nor of the refinements which had comprised, loosely speaking, a town. Navy dive-bombers directed by Lieutenant Commander Bill Beakley were roaring overhead and planting their eggs with pinpoint precision. The enemy of course took to the caves, with only a handful electing to fight it out on top.

Companies B and D organized and quickly worked their way overland through rough country. At the cliffs they met the first concerted enemy resistance. At Hill No. 208 they found that the Japs had dug in and had to be burrowed out with rifle and grenade. Two more Marine companies hit the beach and, spreading out fanshape, took the Jap-infested hills in inch-by-inch fighting, much of it hand-to-hand.

Only three prisoners were taken.

On the tiny harbor island of Gavutu, an offshoot of Tulagi, Major Robert H. Williams, 1st Parachute Battalion waded into the beach amid fiery debris of burning Jap float planes. A five minute 'softening up' job by cruiser *San Juan* and destroyers *Buchanan* and *Monssen* had raised hell at the seaplane base and ramp, demolishing a few three-inch gun emplacements in the process. But the snipers were still rabid. This was immediately translated into a multi-angled crossfire from concealed Kure Marines, as their opposite numbers hit the beach and the Japs let them come. Then, as the men were forming up to clean out the 'ratpacks,' enemy troops opened up from slit trenches, a flanking hill, and tiny *Tanambogo* to the north. Marines hit the beach belly down but one of every ten caught an enemy bullet.

The parachutists quickly spread out and rushed up the hilly terrain, cleaning it out with systematic precision. The few Japs who lived to fight again, died in the caves shortly after. Neighboring Tanambogo got a working over from the dive bombers for ten minutes and not a tree was standing when they cleared the area. Then the

Marines went in from Gavutu, fighting with tanks and reinforcements that cost 108 killed, 140 wounded. Lieutenant Juntaro Maruyama's Marine labor battalion died well.

On the tiny harbor islands of Gavutu and Tanambogo, however, fighting would continue for Marines yet another week, although these would be isolated skirmishes against cave-entrenched holdouts. But in the end all holdouts would be dead.

Considering the size of the task force, D-Day was an altogether successful operation for the United States Navy. During the afternoon, twice, Japanese bombers came down from Rabaul but forewarned by coastwatchers, Allied warships and transports got under way and escaped enemy bombs. This was due in part to the fighter-director team in heavy cruiser *Chicago* which picked up Rear Admiral Yamada's first sortie at 1:15 P.M., distant 43 miles. Then at 3 P.M. the enemy came down again, scoring only one hit and that on destroyer *Mugford,* killing 22 men.

But these counterattacks from Rabaul did nothing to upset Vice Admiral Ghormley's operation. They were initial Japanese reaction, and were ineffectual largely because of precautions—one of which was an effective Combat Air Patrol provided by the three carriers *Saratoga, Essex,* and *Wasp.* The enemy lost about 29 planes to 12 F4Fs and one SBD.

Yamada sent down a flight of 27 bombers the next afternoon, Saturday, but again the transports were clear of their moorings off the beaches. Out of the entire flight 17 were shot down by Navy gunners, and again the cost was comparatively minor: one hit on the destroyer *Jarvis* and a suicide hit on the transport *George F. Elliot,* which was abandoned prematurely by a panicky merchant crew. Flames from her topside fires roared well into the night, a highly significant and ominous symbol of what was to come. Otherwise Saturday was a good day for the Navy. True, there was a good deal of confusion on the beaches and the men were dogtired from standing incessant watches but few complained. The morning was further brightened by a congratulatory speech by Vice Admiral Ghormley at Noumea (nearly 1,000 miles from the scene) to the effect that "results so far achieved make every officer and man in the South Pacific proud of the task forces." The Navy was beat, but happy, and most of the ships in the forces set Condition II which gave half of the crew time for the sack.

So, until sunset, Rear Admiral Turner aboard flagship *McCawley* worried only about Japanese air attacks and unloading his ships' cargos. Retaliation by an enemy task force seemed a remote possibility, for air searches flown by Admiral McCain's bombers from the island of Malaita revealed nothing on the sea.

Rear Admiral Mikawa and his staff boarded the heavy cruiser *Chokai* at 2:30 P.M., and in perfect weather got under way to meet the force of warships standing down from Kavieng.

An operations plan—attack the American transports about midnight Sunday—had been radioed earlier to Tokyo and Admiral Osami Nagano, chief of staff, had asserted initially that the scheme was "reckless and dangerous," but nonetheless had given his approval simply because there was no other alternative.

Admiral Mikawa's two-starred flag was flying smartly from the yard of the heavy cruiser, his flagship, as she steamed southward in St. George's Channel at 28 knots. The sea was flat calm, and the sky was brassy with sunlight. Throughout the ship there was a feeling of great confidence and determination, for in night attack there was no fleet the equal of the Imperial Japanese Navy. However, none of the ships with the exception of those

24

of Crudiv 6 had ever operated together and Mikawa's staff had certain reservations about the effectiveness of attack under these conditions. The admiral shrugged this off:

"The commander of each ship is a skilled veteran," he declared. "Maximum effectiveness can be achieved by single-column formation."

Not long after passing out of the harbor, lookouts reported pagoda masts on the horizon. These were *Aoba, Kako, Kinugasa, Furutaka,* and their screening ships, who fell into line without incident and assumed cruising disposition upon receipt of a signal from the flagship. It was an uneventful dusk and a peaceful evening, unmarred despite the detection of an American submarine (S-28; Lieutenant Commander H. G. Munson commanding) on the surface 15 miles east of the New Ireland coast.

After avoiding the submarine which, shortly after, sent off the first contact report of a Japanese task force, Admiral Mikawa settled down to planning the actual attack. The speed of the eight-ship task force was now increased to 30 knots and Mikawa, who had been on the bridge since leaving Rabaul, retired to his sea cabin. Here, according to his staff, he offered a tea toast to the gilt-framed picture of Emperor Hirohito and prayed for Divine guidance, after which he carefully wrote out his battle orders, and called it a night.

The course of the task force was north by east, shaping north of Buka, and thence down through The Slot—eight ships with an aggregate total firepower of 34 8-inch (20 cm) guns; 10 5.5-inch (14 cm) guns; 27 5-inch and 4.7-inch guns; and 62 torpedo tubes. In addition, there were two searchlights aboard each ship, fore and aft. Japanese night gunnery, which was soundly built on the principle of years of fleet maneuvers, was second to none. Her lookouts, without night glasses, could spot the loom of a ship in the darkness at four miles; Japanese torpedoes were far superior to the enemy's: the dreaded "Long Lance" for example, with its 24-inch diameter could carry 1,000 pounds of TNT 11 miles at 49 knots compared with American 'fish' whose warheads accommodated 750 pounds at 45 knots for a distance of 3 miles, and also Japanese binoculars were far superior to anything possessed by the Americans.

Mikawa slept well, and with the knowledge that his quaint looking task force led by *Chokai* was on its way to certain engagement. Perhaps even decisive engagement. The flagship, triple-hulled and displacing 10,000 tons, was 600 feet long. Her forward fat stack curled back and almost hit the risers of the thin second stack. Pagoda masts bristling from the larger ships in the force gave them that 'housing development' look which appeared amusing in retrospect but which was not very amusing to men who faced them as enemies. All bridges bristled with antiaircraft and smaller automatic guns.

Yubari and *Tenryu*, left and right respectively, rode ahead of the flagship on either flank and at a distance of two miles. The other ships were spaced out at 1,000 meter intervals, and from each stack streamed a single white pennant which fluttered in the night and was aloft for purposes of distinguishing friendly ships in time of battle.

Reveille came early for Mikawa. Awakened by an orderly at 5:15 the admiral was brought a pot of tea and told that float planes were about to fly off on scouting missions. Mikawa dressed quickly and went up on the bridge to watch the launchings. Standing with his staff, silent and stony-faced, he witnessed the first of six catapults send off the winged messengers of reconnaissance. Then, with his staff, he retired to the wardroom for breakfast. All hands said a prayer for the pilots, asking for a safe journey and that the enemy would still be concentrated at Guadalcanal and Tulagi. The air was heavy with anxiety and hopefulness befitting the occasion, punctuated occasionally by light banter which concealed nothing. Mikawa, after breakfast, went up to the *Chokai*'s Combat Intelligence Center, to busy himself with the myriads of details of the task force while keeping one ear on the aircraft frequency.

No word from the planes came for approximately four hours. Shortly before voices of jubilant pilots wheezed over the air, the admiral, having gone out to the open bridge, was staring at the open sea ahead and pacing furiously. *Chokai*'s skipper, Captain Masami Ban, who was in CIC during the hours from 8 to 10 between short excursions to the pilot house, rushed to Mikawa's side.

"They have found them!" he beamed elatedly. "The airwaves are wild with the sound of them—"

The little admiral rushed into the crowded compartment as pilots voices' squealed that there were "fifteen transports to the north," and a few seconds later, flying over Tulagi, "two enemy heavy cruisers, twelve destroyers, and three transports."

But the joy of finding the enemy was shortlived. Quickly the staff went to work analyzing the messages and above all else, one thing was fairly obvious: for some reason there were no American carriers in the vicinity and this was a great disappointment to the attacking force. Mikawa's staff could hear the American carrier pilots speaking in plain language. Yet they had withdrawn —where were they now? While Mikawa was coming to grips with this problem, and it was one with serious undertones, still another developed.

Out of the halcyon sky burst a Hudson bomber at 10:26, a dark shadow against the curtain of puffball blue. The aircraft, Australian, circled the task force for some minutes and then disappeared. Staff officers interpreted this as a coming of terrible things, for now that the force had been spotted *anything* could happen, including an alert enemy waiting for them and/or a carrier plane at tack. While considering these unpalatable possibilities, a second bomber, Australian, far bolder than his predecessor, burst through cloud cover to make a pass at *Chokai*. Main battery fire finally drove off this intruder. However, by now the admiral was worried to distraction, although his staff was not.

Irrespective of enemy planes, they felt, there was a large task force demanding of their attention and good samurais that they were they wanted to attack. Mikawa's zeal was tempered, on the other hand, by simple logic and, not wanting his column of ships to be battered to extinction by a superior force in one fell swoop, he divided his ships so that a sizable portion of them remained in a rear position many thousands of meters astern. The long day wore on but nothing happened by way of new excitement. Mikawa, of course, was worried—although to his men he presented a picture of absolute confidence and one which inspired complete faith down to the lowliest rating. A sturdy figure in blue striding the open bridge, composed and self-assured, inwardly Mikawa was a seething knot of emotions. *Turn back or keep going? What about those planes? Was a trap waiting at Guadalcanal?* Time only would unravel the dilemma.

The task force moved southward at 24 knots, almost a leisurely pace, timing its arrival at the invasion points for midnight. At 4:30 Mikawa ordered a flag hoist for his battle plan and the wondrous words stood out vividly against the flawless sky: "We will penetrate south of Savo Sound and torpedo the enemy main force at Guadalcanal. Thence we will move toward the forward area at Tulagi and strike with torpedoes and gunfire, after which we will withdraw to the north of Savo Island."

The serenity of Mikawa's column was shaken when lookouts detected masts on the horizon. However, luck was riding with Mikawa this dusk and the ship turned out to be a friendly (*Akitsushima of Eleventh Fleet*) vessel en route to Vella Gulf. There were no other close calls. At 6:30 sailors dressed themselves in colorful bandanas and handkerchiefs-around-foreheads, stripped ships for night action, while they listened to the exhortations of gun captains in final briefings. It was as if all ships companies knew that their admiral's luck was going to hold this night. Just before dark Captain Ohmae, Mikawa's chief of staff, drafted a message to the force:

"In the finest tradition of the Imperial Navy, we shall engage the enemy in night battle. May each one calmly do his utmost."

It was 7 P.M.

At an RAAF base in Australia, the pilot of the first Hudson which had spotted Mikawa at 10:15 that morning, was setting down on a runway. When the plane came to a stop the pilot walked into the ready room, had a cup of tea and then—*8 hours after sighting the Japanese force*—reported the southbound enemy ships. This report was put on the RAAF equivalent of the "Fox" Sked and routinely radioed to all the ships at sea. Yet even this was incorrectly reported: "Three cruisers, three destroyers, two seaplane tenders or gunboats, course 120°, speed 15 knots."

The second Hudson didn't bother to report.

S-38's advance warning of a Japanese force had come in almost 16 hours before, but searches over a wide area had completely missed Mikawa. It was an uneasy Saturday night for Rear Admiral Turner, worsened by the fact that at 6:15 Vice Admiral Fletcher passed a "recommend withdrawal" message to Vice Admiral Ghormley.

"Fighter strength reduced from 99 to 78. In view of the large number of enemy torpedo planes and bombers in this area, I recommend . . ."

Fletcher, roundly criticized for this message to Commander, South Pacific Area and Force, had lost *Lexington* at Coral Sea and *Yorktown* at Midway. He had fought in every engagement since Pearl Harbor and his weariness was readily understandable. Without waiting for a reply, Fletcher barreled off to the southeast with his task force and Turner was left without air support.

Turner of course was furious. In his words, he'd been caught "bare-arse." The situation was urgent so far as he was concerned and he passed the information of a possible night engagement along to his respective commanders. He also arranged for a meeting aboard flagship *McCawley* with Rear Admiral Crutchley and Major General Vandergrift.

So things stood as nightfall descended on the Solomons.

The immediate problem, defense of Turner's transports, fell now to Rear Admiral Crutchley, the Englishman who was aboard his flagship HMAS *Australia*. Crutchley divided his patrolling forces in three groups: Northern, Southern and Eastern, a mighty screen of warships built around cruisers and destroyers which, on paper, at least, could stop any penetration by the enemy.

These forces moved into cruising disposition after dark, the Northern Force, with Captain Frederick Riefkohl commanding aboard *Vincennes*, consisting also of *Astoria* (Captain William G. Greenman) and *Quincy* (Captain Samuel N. Moore). Destroyers *Wilson* and *Helm* (Lieutenant Commanders Walter H. Price and Chester E. Carrol, respectively) served as screen and were positioned on the port and starboard flanks of the heavy cruisers whose *raison d'etre* was the blocking "of the entrance between Savo and Florida Islands." Radar pickets *Ralph Talbot* and *Blue* were stationed at both approaches of Savo Sound.

Captain Howard D. Bode, skipper of the *Chicago*, was in command of the Southern Force in the absence of Rear Admiral Crutchley who, at 9 A.M., would be en route to Turner's meeting on board the *McCawley*. This meeting would pull *Australia* out of the line, leaving only one heavy cruiser and a destroyer screen consisting of *Bagley* (Lieutenant Commander George A. Sinclair) and *Patterson* (Commander Frank R. Walker). Their patrol was a line "running 125 degrees from the center of Savo Island to block the entrance between it and Cape Esperance."

Eastern Force, which would miss entirely the action this fateful night, was commanded by Rear Admiral Norman Scott in light cruiser *San Juan*, and composed of destroyers *Buchanan* (Commander Ralph E. Wilson) and *Monssen* (Captain Roland M. Smoot). Also in company was HMAS *Hobart* (Captain Henry A. Showers RAN).

This was the precise structure of the transport screen as darkness fell and low-scudding thunder heads turned the night pitch black "with a dank, wet eerie feeling persisting on the bridges of ships." Condition II, which allowed half of ships' crews to hit the sack, was set and so, with no battle plan for there hadn't been time for Crutchley to formulate one, the ships patrolled on station.

At 9 P.M., with weather thickening in the Sound, the British admiral pulled HMAS *Australia* out of the line and barreled inshore to Turner's flagship, *McCawley*, to attend a conference. Only Vandergrift, the Marine general, Turner and Crutchley were present. These were tired, haggard men who were meeting in emergency session to discuss the effect 1) of Fletcher's withdrawal and 2) the possibility of unloading transports all night and beating a hasty exit from Guadalcanal and Tulagi in the morning. Of this parliament Vandergrift later remarked, "I was beat, but as for those other two, I thought they were both ready to pass out."

Turner, exhausted from two days of more or less incessant bombing raids, presented his recommendations for withdrawal to which Vandergrift reacted strongly. Who would protect his Marines? he asked. Did Turner realize that 20,000 men would be left to their own devices on a strange beach with little or no supplies? And so the arguments went, strong and just on either side, while the warships aware that the Japs were coming down "in force" crept stealthily along the boundaries of their patrol areas.

Of the three groups, only the Southern Force of ships had ever operated together. The two others were working "by guess and by God." Captain Howard Bode, who became OTC (Officer in Tactical Command) when Crutchley departed for the meeting, and a man who would take his own life as a result of this night, saw no point in changing *Chicago*'s position behind *Australia* as he believed that the British Admiral would return before long. So piled up the first of a long, fatal series of mistakes. A capable officer and a veteran of "the Anzac Force," a group of warships which materially assisted in the defense of Australia when the Japanese threat to that strategic area was a daily thing, Bode, CO of the *Chicago*, alerted his crew of the possibility of enemy attack and let things pretty much run themselves after that.

Captain Frederick Riefkohl, winner of a Navy Cross for action in World War I when his gun crew had driven off a German U-boat, was in command of the Northern Force aboard the heavy cruiser *Vincennes*. While his men were at Condition II, Riefkohl—"affable and good admiral material according to his juniors"—had advised his officers of the possibility of enemy attack and had written in the night order book that utmost caution should be exercised while on patrol. A formidable group of ships at his command, Riefkohl wasn't particularly worried as he slipped into his sea cabin for a few winks. His powerful squadron, thought he, could handle anything Japanese.

Thus passed the early night, Mikawa barrelling down The Slot and three U.S. groups obliviously patrolling in

Savo Sound some 1,500 yards apart on station. All was well . . . and all was black except where the transport *Elliot,* flaming and burning "like a beacon" was silhouetting Turner's transports. On the harbor islands of Gavutu and Tanambogo, tracer trails indicated still some fighting with the Kure Marines, but other than this slight nuisance there was no indication of trouble anywhere. An aircraft was heard on HMAS *Canberra* and picked up on Type 271 RDF (Mikawa's float planes) but nobody on the bridge bothered to make a fuss about this. The consensus was that American destroyers had a Jap sub pinned down at the roadstead and were depth charging.

Nothing more.

Mikawa, meanwhile, was coming with a bone in his teeth: all ships steaming at 26 knots and stripped down for night action, flying ghostly white pennants which streamed from ships' funnels for identification purposes during the heat of the fray; all ships of his task force riding in a single column 1,200 meters apart. At 11:10, the Japanese admiral, hoping to learn more of the enemy conglomeration at Guadalcanal and Tulagi, had launched five float-type aircraft from his cruisers. After a tense 20 minutes, during which the task force passed in and out of rain squalls, the admiral was called to *Chokai's* chart room radio by Captain Masami Ban, the CO. A message was coming in:

"Three enemy cruisers patrolling off the eastern entrance of Savo Sound!"

Mikawa crossed his fingers and upped the task force's speed to 28 knots. Electric tension coursed through the command as half-naked gunners licked their chops in greedy anticipation—*four cruisers!* And how many more elsewhere in Savo Sound? Other pilot reports streamed into the flagship. The admiral now betook himself to the bridge to command the final approach.

He had no radar; only the eyes of his magnificently

trained lookouts would spot the loom of American targets in a body of water which, after tonight, fighting men would evermore call Ironbottom Sound. The little admiral sucked in his breath and waited. Then, at 12:40, another report, as the truncated cone of Savo Island appeared on the horizon. This one came from a wingtip of the flagship, and it was spat out like a destroyer firing torpedoes:

"Ship approaching thirty degrees starboard!"

Mikawa pulled up his binoculars. In CIC (Combat Intelligence Center) the admiral's staff, hearing the sighting report, immediately considered the possibility of attacking this vessel at once. But the plucky Mikawa said he wanted to gamble, and so it was that an American tin can passed at 10,000 meters while a thousand guns were trained on her ready to fire at the slightest wrong move. Then, a moment later, another shocker, even before the effects of the first had worn away:

"Ship sighted, twenty degrees port!"

Mikawa swiveled sharply.

"Right rudder!" he snapped. "Steer course one five oh degrees!"

Another American destroyer—even closer.

The guns trained 'round, but again the enemy ship was silent and it glided through the murky night without opening fire. The minutes dragged. Mikawa ordered speed increased to 30 knots. He detached *Yanagi* at 1:30 to attack the American destroyers so recently passed. Then, in rapid succession, new reports from the lookouts:

"Cruiser, seven degrees port!—"Three cruisers, nine degrees starboard, moving to right!"

Mikawa passed the word for the planes to drop their parachute flares and instantly the night was illuminated in an eerie red brilliance. Range: 8,000 meters. Captain Ban stood beside his admiral, a stolid figure waiting to relay the long delayed order, but the admiral wasn't ready quite yet. Seven frenetic minutes would elapse before Gunichi Mikawa's command lashed *Chokai*'s crowded bridge.

Exactly at 1:47 it came: "Torpedoes fire to starboard —*fire!*"

In the Southern Force, first to feel the wrath of the Imperial Japanese Navy was HMAS *Canberra,* Captain Frank "Ting" Getting commanding.

Aloft on the foremast of the 9,850 ton cruiser was Able Seaman Mackintosh, one of the lookouts who was squinting into the drizzle, having just come up for the 12-to-4 watch. Mackintosh suddenly tensed as the shape of a vessel, bow on, rammed into focus. But before the lookout could speak, torpedo tracks were slashing down on both sides. He stared in horror at the horizon ahead which was bathed in brilliant orange-yellow flame—*gunfire!*

Mackintosh screamed: "Torpedoes both sides! Gunfire dead on the starboard bow!"

At about this moment flares drifted downward, lighting in ghostly relief the forms of cruisers *Chicago* and *Canberra,* with the transports in the background at anchorage. Lieutenant Commander David Mesley, OOD, in the pilot house, hit the general alarm and immediately *Canberra* went to Battle Stations. But it was too late. Mikawa's fish were at the end of their track and the ones to starboard scored; a moment later, the first of 24 heavy-caliber shells *wrranged* through the high-hulled cruiser.

Out from the pilot house streaked Captain Getting. He had been catching "a few winks" in his emergency cabin and was on his feet, racing to the bridge, a few seconds after the torpedo hit. At 43 Getting, capable and conscientious, was one of the youngest RAN officers bucking for rear admiral. He was, in fact, slated for promotion to this grade in a few months. A veteran of the Pacific war since its earliest days and before Getting, on the China Station in peacetime, had nearly caused an international incident by overhauling a Russian freighter carrying a contraband cargo . . . in the wake of a similar feat involving Japanese nationals. "Ting" Getting had earned a fighter's reputation when, in the spring of 1942, after three years' duty at the War Department, he received command of *Canberra* and took the cruiser on convoy tours of the Indian Ocean.

As gunnery officer Lieutenant Commander Hole shouted for main batteries to train out and commence firing, Getting raced to his side. Mikawa's steel fists were now beginning to batter *Canberra* to oblivion. The proud warship, built in 1928 under the Naval Armament Treaty Agreement, was utterly unable to defend herself in the teeth of the onslaught.

Shells screamed in along her topsides and superstructure, starting fires, immediately causing a loss of electricity to her directors. Then another catastrophe—complete loss of power. *Canberra* was lost and those white-clad officers crowding her bridge knew it only too well as men began to die throughout the warship.

The rain of hammer blows fell on the bridge, pilot house, plotting room and wings as *Canberra*, crawling dazedly in her own wake, attempted the manual fire of her dwindling main battery. Captain Getting, directing his guns at the enemy dead ahead, with the navigator and gunnery officer closeby, fell to the deck mortally wounded as an 8-inch shell from *Choakai* ploughed into the compartment. There were five enlisted ratings present who also sagged to the deck as if their legs had been clipped by the swift stroke of the Devil's scythe. Heavy black smoke boiled up and shrouded the bloody, fallen bodies of *Canberra*'s command, and where the shell had actually hit there was now a blaze of fiery light from which individual yellow tongues of flame danced along the overhead.

Commander James A. Walsh, the cruiser's executive officer who was battling his way to the bridge from after control, came upon this scene of death and destruction in which he found his commanding officer. A helmsman was struggling to his feet, blood spanking out of a hole in his shoulder. Walsh, now joined by ship's doctors Downward and Warder, did their utmost to restrain Getting but the commanding officer insisted on being placed on his stool and directing the fight.

Reports streamed up to the bridge that the engine rooms were afire and filled with dead, while out on deck gunners said that the ready rooms were beginning to explode from the heat alone. Fifty foot flames millraced back from the bow to the fantail, between which were the blackened corpses of the cruiser's deck force. Yet this floating charnal house lived on a little longer, occasionally grinding out a shot from one battery and a few automatic guns, and her jagged torpedo holes now assumed a hard starboard list.

"Jim, fight her till she goes down!" Getting, the life slowly beginning to ebb from his torn body, whispered to Commander Walsh.

The Exec did just that.

Japanese torpedoes and gunfire mercilessly raked this proud vessel, ripping her asunder as if she was made of shredded paper, buckling her decks, and spewing her dead and wounded along blood-gutted decks and blackened passageways. Four-inch shells and 1.1 ammo began to explode in a staccato and deafening millrace of flame along her topsides. But her crew fought her to the end as bloody, half-dead sailors crept out of the miring black smoke and staggered to the railings with hot shells which they heaved overboard in a last, unavailing effort to prevent the cruiser from blowing herself up.

Mikawa's column of ships turned their attention next to *Chicago*, the first 8-inch shell from the flagship neatly clipping the starboard leg of the foremast and knocking out XGE Cable to the No. 1 director. A Japanese Long Lance smashed into the bow and ripped away everything to Frame No. 4, the whole shapeless mass suddenly hanging there like a man swinging from the gallows. On the bridge, Captain Howard Bode suddenly appeared and ordered the OOD to have the searchlights snapped on. His cruiser was responding with starshells—44 of them—attempting to light the enemy. Bode's warship, however, needed none—and neither would any other Allied vessel who would taste Mikawa's bitter tea this night!

On the catapults, float plane No. 0388 was blazing along its diagonals (*Canberra*'s two Walrus scout jobs were likewise a bonfire to fire fighting parties) and monstrous flames were soaring high above the superstructure.

The cataclysm of death rolled on. Mikawa had opened fire at 7,200 yards and had now closed to 4,000. In *Chicago*'s sickbay, the ship's dentist, Dr. Benjamin Ostering was operating on Commander Cecil C. Adell, the executive officer, for wounds received in the neck. In the main operating room a young seaman, Arthur Cornelius Ryan, was about to undergo the amputation of his left leg. Throughout the heavy cruiser men were falling in pathetic heaps around their guns as Bode, who had ordered illumination by searchlight, could not only find friendly targets—American destroyer *Patterson*, the first ship to fire on Mikawa and the first to be fired upon in return.

Admiral Mikawa's forces had come, struck, and vanished by 1:44 A.M. *Chokai* was bearing down on the Northern Force of ships on course zero six eight. His eight-ship force (minus *Yunagi* which had been detached earlier) was inadvertently splitting formation so that *Aoba*, *Chokai*, *Kako* and *Kinugasa* rode together in column, and *Yubari, Tenryu* and *Furutaka* in a second column.

The twin-tailed sea monster bore down at full speed on the Northern Force led by cruiser *Astoria*. Lieutenant Commander James R. Topper, the damage control officer, was on the bridge serving as supervisor of the watch. Captain William G. Greenman, a lean, pleasant man from Watertown, N.Y., was in his emergency cabin abaft the bridge having left similar orders as his opposite numbers to "wake me if anything happens."

Topper, 34, noted in *Astoria*'s log a few minutes before *Chokai*'s 36-inch searchlight snapped on and shells began to fall: "Steaming on intercardinal courses at ten knots. Sea smooth, visibility fair. Ceiling down about 1,500 feet, except around Savo Island." At Condition II, only seven of her boilers were on the line—clear indication that Captain Greenman—as all others—expected nothing of significance to occur before morning when the enemy task force would be within striking distance of Guadalcanal and Tulagi.

At 1:36 A.M. Topper had been on the bridge almost two hours. Neither he, nor any other OODS of the Northern Force, had heard a TBS warning by destroyer *Patterson*, a picket, that "strange ships are entering the harbor!" So, then, the watch was a quiet one, without special tension, with the men on the bridge occasionally remarking about Japanese resistance on Tulagi ("they're having a helluva time there") but nothing else.

Lieutenant Commander William H. Truesdell, the gunnery officer, was napping on the sky control station platform. He, too, had given orders to "wake me if anything happens," and at 1:44 A.M., when the first of Mikawa's starshells burst over Savo Sound, a sailor shook him conscious. Truesdell immediately bolted upright and saw four of the shells falling astern.

"Tell the bridge to sound the general alarm!"

39

Truesdell snapped, while below on the bridge Topper saw the same incredible sight and quickly dispatched a messenger to wake Captain Greenman. Then Truesdell ordered the quarter-master to sound the general alarm. Flares signified enemy action and six 8-inch guns, the first to be fired by an American cruiser in the Northern Force, sundered the night. At this moment the commanding officer appeared on the bridge and, sprinting to the starboard wing where his supervisor of the watch and several others were standing, immediately pounced on Topper:

"Who sounded the general alarm? Who gave the order to commence firing?"

Then, a moment later: "Topper, I think we are firing on our own ships. Let's not get excited and act too hastily. Cease firing!"

All gunnery stopped.

The dark silhouettes of the Japanese columns moved closer and in main battery control an officer recognized *Chokai* just as she snapped on her searchlight and started pouring out a deadly fire, Greenman and Topper, startled by the sudden flash of what was obviously a group commencing a broadside, gasped in utter disbelief, while above "Guns" was howling to his telephone talker and now the talker was relaying the message to the bridge:

"Mr. Truesdell said for God's sake give the word to commence firing!"

The dilemma on the bridge of this doomed 9,950 ton cruiser was tantamount to a glass of saki for the onrushing Japanese. They were slashing away with gunfire and torpedoes, with no return fire from the enemy! Greenman, troubled by the show of searchlights and gunfire, sadly shook his head and, still believing that it was all one big horrible mistake, observed:

40

"Whether they're our ships or not, we will have to stop them. Commence firing!"

At this moment the first of *Chokai*'s eight-inchers came aboard and, piercing the hangar where flat planes were stored, instantly turned that area into a raging bonfire. Mikawa snapped off his lights in satisfaction—the three American cruisers were well lighted! On *Astoria,* executive officer Commander Frank E. Shoup was racing down a ladder to control aft when the shells started coming. Concussion spilled him flat on his face, the net result of which was a badly broken leg and severe shrapnel burns. The catapult and its planes were burning too, and Shoup after an heroic effort to toss flaming debris over the side while hobbling on one leg, collapsed. Mikawa, at 6,000 yards, put *Astoria*'s Turret 3 out of commission and a short time later when Mikawa decided to illuminate again "just to ascertain position of these targets," Turret I.

The black hand of death now quickly pressed down on Greenman's cruiser, as sailors in Turret I, both chamber and upper powder rooms, fell victims to the first Japanese shells. Geysers of water leaped up around the stricken vessel as Japanese gunners, correcting their marksmanship, moved to greater accuracy.

In central control, now filled with pungent black smoke and flying sparks along the bulkheads, Topper recorded: "A shell exploded directly above us. Seaman 1/c T. C. Halligan grabbed the CO_2 extinguisher and played it on the debris, but this room was a death trap filled with large pieces of hot sparking metal, burning rubber and debris dropping on deck."

The Northern Force, speed upped to 15 knots, maneuvered wildly as all hell broke loose. *Astoria,* in danger of collision with *Quincy* which was flaming from bow to stern by now, came to full left rudder.

41

Greenman, on the bridge of his gallant cruiser, was fighting mad—too late. Enemy shells had already started to make of his ship a crematorium.

Vincennes, command vessel of this formation, suffered her fatal drubbing by Mikawa in exactly 18 minutes.

Ironically, this warship had carried the ashes of Japan's foreign minister to the United States back to his homeland in 1939. A comparatively new cruiser with the latest in fire power, *Vinny Maru*, as her devoted crew of a thousand called her, had also been the victim of indecision and lethargy when Mikawa presented his calling card.

Lieutenant Commander Craighill, assistant gunnery officer, was standing in the pilot house sweeping the sea with his glasses at 1:43 A.M. when a flash of light "which might have been gunfire lighted the sky for an instant." As four stars burst on his port quarter, Craighill told the OOD to wake the captain. An instant later, the sky which to this moment had been leaden and squally, brightened under the flash of Japanese main battery. In main battery control, Commander R. L. Adams—"Guns" —saw the shells at the same instant. All reports streamed into the bridge as a messenger raced to awaken Captain Riefkohl in his emergency cabin. There was no indecision on Riefkohl's part for he, of all the officers afloat, truly anticipated trouble.

"Commence firing!" Riefkohl roared.

Adams, on the control platform above the bridge, responded with an order to his gunners to train out to port and let fly.

Then Riefkohl, seeing a searchlight's glare on the water close aboard, angrily ordered the light doused (*Chokai*'s), thinking they were his own, but instead of compliance which he fully expected, Riefkohl saw the first giant water spouts resulting from *Kako's* initial salvo. Range was down to 8,250 yards as that miss was recorded at 500 yards. *Vinny Maru,* charging angrily at the light, slammed out a full salvo (her second) at the silhouette which was *Kinugasa.* In the next moment, as Japanese gunnery began to tell, her salvos fell off sharply. The enemy's first sheels screamed aboard in the vicinity of the hangars and well deck; a movie projection booth burst into flame and the nearby stores of aviation gasoline. Flames, quickly licking their way greedily over the after end of the warship, jumped to a ladder to where Commander W. E. A. Mullen, the exec, was coming down and Mullen, braving the flames, raced aft to start the fire pumps and direct fire fighting teams.

In the pilot house, Captain Riefkohl was watching with growing dissatisfaction and alarm, his own salvos falling away to token firing. His first reaction was to order an increase of speed to 20 knots "to close the enemy" with the "wheel put over hard left." However, at this moment disaster overtook the bridge of the *Vincennes.* A direct hit was sustained by the bridge which killed and wounded a great number of the personnel there and knocked out communications both to her own engine rooms and to the other warships of the Northern Force. With steering now reduced to "the white pointer," *Vinny Maru* made her emergency turn.

Astoria and *Quincy,* captained by former destroyer men as was Riefkohl, turned instinctively. But the execution of this maneuver was of no avail. Japanese fire, murderously accurate as the range came down to 4,000 yards, deluged the *Vincennes* with 85 major caliber shells fired point blank.

All power to gun turrets failed. On the signal bridge, the flag bags burst into flame. Hits streamed into Main Radio knocking out radar, radio transmitters, communications, and scattering bluejackets in a welter of sudden death. In the turrets themselves, the hoists became instantly inoperative as enemy fire raked her lengthwise down the starboard side. Finally, both engine rooms became "black and dead." All guns were out of commission. Her ensign, shot away by enemy gunners who redoubled their efforts at the sight of "an Admiral's flag" was now, under great hazard, replaced with a new one by Chief Signalman George J. Moore who braved their murderous fire.

Death slewed across the gun decks with rapier swiftness, mowing down the crews of 5-inch and smaller, and finally closing in from the sea with a heavy list to port. *Vincennes* gagged in her death throes.

Cruiser *Quincy*, 9375-tons, was mortally wounded almost at the same moment. Like the others, Captain Samuel N. Moore, upon hearing the alarm, rushed out from his emergency cabin where he had been napping, in time to see starshells falling over Savo Sound. Commander Edward E. Billings, supervisor of the watch, told the captain as he stormed out in time to see strange ships illuminating, "They're not ours, sir!"

But Moore had a distinctly different reaction, probably the only commanding officer to so react. "Fire on the searchlights!" he roared. "Commence firing!"

Quincy, boiling up now at 15 knots, turned on recognition lights even as her main battery boomed in salvo. But the principle that it was better to be safe than sorry availed her nothing. Mikawa bowed politely and identified himself with steel-spitting main batteries. Whose ships were those? Was it some kind of drill? Men at strategic stations, among them Lieutenant Commander H. B. Henneberger who would soon become *Astoria's* ranking survivor, were still pondering the mystery when the terrible truth emerged from the murk of Savo Sound.

Captain Moore, following OTC's lead, swung his ship hard over to comply with Riefkohl's maneuver and as he was doing this Japanese shells ripped into his cruiser's catapults setting the float jobs afire. Now Mikawa's gunners licked their chops and poured it on. Instantly Director 1 went out. Turret 3 took a direct hit after jamming in train, killing all hands. A hailstorm of raking fire deluged the 1.1 and 40-mm mounts, battering these guns and all personnel to oblivion. The few who crawled away terribly wounded, collapsed on deck and died in the bonfires.

Then, at this moment, *Quincy's* bridge took a direct hit.

Across the wildly lighted waters cruiser *Astoria* was the victim of a shell on her bridge forward of the emergency cabin, a hit which knocked out communications and killed a half-dozen men. Greenman, unhurt save for shrapnel wounds, staggered to the wheel where Quartermaster 1/c R. Williams lay dead at the feet of Boatswain's Mate 1/c J. Young, himself severely wounded. Greenman started to grab the wheel but Quartermaster 2/c R. A. Radke was there and grabbed it himself.

"I think we're on 185 degrees," croaked Young. "Stay with it—"

He did.

On the boat deck the motor launches now caught hell. Wooden boats, hammered by the falling shells quickly turned to kindling and, in turn, to a holocaust. The gun decks, too, where 5-inch ammo was stored in ready boxes, caught fire and began to explode. Men lay in grotesque piles around the twisted steel of their weapons pleading for help, but there was no help. In Radio I all hands were dead and in the plotting room, pungent black smoke required the survivors there to don gas masks in order to remain at station. Up forward, Lieutenant Commander Walker B. Davidson was climbing on Turret II to direct fire visually when electric control was shot away.

Astoria, dead in the water, flaming from one end of

45

her to the other, lasted out the terrible night alone with her dead and wounded.

Vincennes, down by the head and sinking fast, gave her few survivors time to get on deck for an orderly abandonment. Captain Riefkohl, orderly Corporal J. L. Patrick and Chief Yeoman L. E. Stucker were the last to leave the ship. The three men went around the deck to see if there was anyone yet alive and then, only after they were sure that there wasn't, calmly stepped overboard and into the deep body of water which would henceforth be called Ironbottom Sound. *Vincennes,* blazing fiercely amidships, went down at 2:50 A.M.

Quincy, caught in a crossfire of the two Japanese columns, had succumbed fifteen minutes earlier. Captain Sam Moore, in the pilot house, where a direct hit had been sustained, died with most of his bridge crew. Then, in rapid succession, all his guns were quickly silenced and the holes in his ship began to admit the sea. Lieutenant Commander Henneberger, realizing the utter futility of trying to save her, told a subordinate to order all hands over the side. So it was. *Quincy's* fighting skipper lay a corpse in her battered bridge, one of 332 men aboard her to succumb to Mikawa's fateful visit this night.

Admiral Gunichi Mikawa snapped off his searchlights and started moving out of Savo Sound, work done beyond even his wildest expectations. Only one small chore remained for the jubilant enemy columns barreling out virtually intact, with minor damage sustained by a few ships including *Chokai,* the flagship, victim of an 8-inch shell in her chart room. This was American destroyer *Ralph Talbot.* As the tiny silhouette of the tin can loomed in the darkness at radar range of 3,300-yards, Mikawa ordered light cruiser *Ubari* to "dispose of that" while he hastily reformed the task force. And *Talbot,* victim of an earlier mauling in what to her was a two-part battle, now suddenly was sundered by three Long Lances which set her ablaze, knocked out director control, the No. 4 gun and turned her into a floating junk heap with a 20 degree starboard list.

There was much discussion on the Japanese flagship as to whether they should go back and attack the American transports. But Mikawa, who would be criticized in time for "a lack of initiative" was fearful that Fletcher's aircraft would catch him in The Slot and his stunning victory would be overshadowed by tragic defeat. (Mikawa had no way of knowing that the American vice admiral was hauling off to the south at this very moment and that he could attack transports with impunity.) Thus far he had come away with 35 dead and 51 wounded, a trifling matter when considered in the light of what might have been.

At 2:33 A.M. his signal was flashed from *Chokai's* yard: "All ships withdraw. Force in line, course 320 degrees, speed 30 knots."

He might have added "and let's not push our luck . . ."

American destroyers fared horrendously this night too. *Bagley* (Commander George A. Sinclair) had had a brief encounter when steaming with the Southern Force in the opening phase of the battle. When enemy ships came in range Sinclair, torpedo primers not inserted, made quick adjustments and fired four fish. Four timed explosions, possibly 'end of runs' were heard by Torpedoman 3/c Edward Ryan. Then, for reasons still not clear, *Bagley* hauled off and 'lost' the battle.

Destroyer *Blue* (Commander H. N. Williams) had even worse luck if such was possible. Patrolling on a line west of Savo with his radar gear functioning properly, *Blue* passed close aboard to Mikawa's ships without detecting them. The only thing that this destroyer caught as a result of her sweeps was an intercoastal tramp carrying a native crew and coconuts! Perhaps, as has been pointed out, her mistakes were due to an inexperienced radar operator who was confused by the 'pips' caused by the islands themselves, but in any event nothing deterred *Blue* from her oblivious cruising until called in finally to perform rescue missions.

Helm (Lieutenant Commander Chester E. Carroll) and *Wilson* (Lieutenant Commander Walter H. Price) made precious small contributions to American 'face.' *Helm,* in the vanguard of the Northern Force, looked over her shoulder, as it were, and saw the gun flashes. She barreled back and exhanged shots with a friendly ship and then hauled off again at high speed to run down new phantoms. *Wilson,* firing 200 rounds of 5-inch, at disappearing targets, opened this battle with two mounts which wouldn't train—a lot of noise and no potatoes. *Wilson,* after a near collision with her sister ship, hauled off at 30 knots toward the Savo anchorage.

Only *Ralph Talbot* (Lieutenant Commander Joseph W. Callahan), and then at the end of the battle, acquitted herself well in combat. Destroyer *Jarvis* died the following morning. This ship, which had been hit in the Air raid that same afternoon, was making speed for Australia to effect repairs. She was traveling alone and no doubt saw the Japanese task force, but had no means of communication and was unable to report. Japanese planes of the 25th Air Flotilla, identifying her as an *Achilles*-class cruiser, blasted her to extinction when they came down on the morning raid.

Nearly 1,000 men were in the water at 2:50 A.M. when the main action broke off. *Canberra,* a fiery wreck, was still afloat as was *Astoria,* in similar straits, with her gallant captain and crew attempting vainly to save her. But save her they could not.

What of the commanders—Crutchley and Turner? Crutchley missed the battle of his life. He was returning

48

the Southern Force after a hectic session with Turner aboard the *McCawley*.

"I was in complete ignorance of the number or nature of the enemy force and the progress of the action being fought!" he said later.

And so he was. He learned of the fight by hearing the drumming of guns and seeing the flashes of light over Savo Sound. He learned (to his horror) by calling on TBS the skippers of the *Chicago* and *San Juan*. Little by little, Crutchley—as Turner—learned that hell literally had broken loose and that the only thing possible at this point was an attempt to pick up the pieces.

Destroyers were sent out to search . . . and they found the grisly remains of men and ships. *Canberra*, dispatched to the bottom by a tin can after several unsuccessful attempts, died early Sunday morning. She had battled to the end as her dying commanding officer had ordered. *Astoria's* crew abandoned and then returned, only to fight a losing battle against the sea which continued into noon the following day when Navy rescue tugs decided the venture was hopeless. She rolled over on her beam ends and disappeared slowly, to port, at 12:15 P.M.

Admiral Turner, whose decision was to quit the Solomons, was now frantic to quit before the bombers came down again.

Admiral Fletcher, withdrawing to the south, learned of the battle but refused to head around for his earlier-stated reasons.

Admiral Crutchley, probably talking to himself by now, gathered the last water-logged survivor from Savo Sound.

General Vandergrift? Boiling mad because his troops, with short supplies and no cover, were cast upon these unfriendly islands to await an unwarranted doom.

So went the morning. The evacuation, which began

shortly after the sinking of *Astoria,* culminated some days later in New Caledonia where Vice Admiral Robert L. Ghormley, overall commander of Operation Watchtower, listened incredulously to the tale of horror. Ghormley, who would drag down as large a share of the blame for Savo as any man, did his best to regroup his battered forces. But his best was not nearly good enough.

Four months later, on October 12, the Navy Department released the full story. Still later, an investigating committee headed by Admiral Arthur Hepburn visited the scene and interviewed hundreds of survivors. These findings, still labeled secret after 20 years, are summarized by Rear Admiral Samuel Eliot Morison in his multi-volume *History of U. S. Naval Operations in World War II.* Morison states:

" (a) Inadequate condition of readiness on all ships to meet sudden night attack.

" (b) Failure to recognize the implications of the presence of enemy planes in the vicinity to attack.

" (c) Misplaced confidence in the capabilities of radar installations on *Ralph Talbot* and *Blue.*

" (d) Failure of communications, which resulted in lack of timely receipt of vital enemy contact information.

" (e) Failure in communications . . ."

Admiral Mikawa? That illustrious conqueror hightailed home in a jubilant mood, looking over his shoulder for Fletcher's carrier planes which would never come. Only one short sequel to Savo remained to be played out: *S-44* versus cruiser *Kako.* An American submarine skipper on war patrol off New Britain spotted Mikawa's homeward-bound task force and promptly dispatched pickles on a deadly track. Down by the head went *Kako.*

But the battle—unmistakably a Japanese victory—

.as over. A plucky, iron-nerved son of Heaven had left four cruisers in the graveyard to the southwest. Death toll: 1,024. America would never forget this debacle— nor would Mikawa, soon to rise a notch to vice admiral for his single night's performance.

In Washington, Admiral King, the Chief of Naval Operations, gritted his teeth and accepted these losses philosophically. One could lose the battle and still win the war although, after the Savo debacle, it hardly seemed possible.

PART II

Eastern Solomons

THE EVACUATION of the transports and gun ships from Guadalcanal shortly after noon, August 9, left General Vandergrift's Marines to struggle alone. Short on supplies, without support and naval firepower, the Marine Corps faced up to a bleak future with admirable fortitude. The immediate problem was survival.

Admiral Mikawa had successfully opened the seaway to the islands. He had missed a golden opportunity to strike the transports but had trounced the United States Navy, and it had pulled back. Now the conclusions were obvious to all: Japanese air, surface and submarine forces would, in addition to supplying their beleagured garrison, come down and present fiery calling cards to Vandergrift's intrepid men.

Vandergrift braced himself and planned accordingly.

The marine general set about a three-fold plan which included completion of the airstrip on Guadalcanal, supplying his garrison, and beating down enemy counter-attacks. Morison observes that "if one failed, all failed," which was certainly so. Thus the Marine general, thinking first of survival, set up a five-mile perimeter from Kukum to the Ilu River.

His next step was the use of 90-mm guns to keep the enemy at respectable altitudes; also to capture 3-inch batteries which were turned on submarines soon coming down to bombard. Supplying the Marine garrison was

duced to simple terms—two meals a day including captured Japanese rice—and strictly rationed. So far as the airstrip was concerned, the enemy had left that scar on the face of Guadalcanal's jungle in crudest shape with little more of it finished than a mere clearing of the area.

But Vandergrift had the men and aviation stuffs to get the airstrip built and operational, and he set about it with grim determination. For inspiration, if any was needed, his Marines had before them a tough, leathery soldier-in-the-field operating with them in the hub-deep gunk of Guadalcanal.

On August 15, Vice Admiral Ghormley's promised reinforcements arrived and Marines were cheered by the sight of destroyer-transports *Calhoun*, *Gregory*, *Little* and *McKean* closing the beach through Ironbottom Sound. Aboard were bombs, aviation gas and approximately 150 men of Cub One, the latter to help build the airstrip which Marines would name Henderson Field in memory of a Marine flier lost at Midway. Much of the bitterness felt by the Marine Corps since Turner's pullout, evanesced in a welter of feverish activity and full stomachs. Again, on the 20th, three APDs steamed into Jap-controlled waters to bring Marines a scant 100 tons of supplies—not much considering the number of American Marines to feed but a pretty good starter.

In Rabaul, fresh from Tokyo's tea houses, was Lieutenant General Haruoshi Hyakutate, commander of the Nineteenth Army. Unlike Vandergrift, Hyakutate was a book man who lived by the Imperial manual. The manual told him that "the character of the American is simple and lacking in tenacity and battle leadership . . . if they have a setback, they have a tendency to abandon one plan for another . . ."

Hyakutate's Army, then in the gathering stage and composed of crack combat units stationed in China, Philippines, Singapore and Borneo, numbered on paper some 50,000 men. Most of them shared their general's low opinion of the American enemy. American Marines, estimated at 10,000 in the Solomons, could likely be further set back by throwing in a mere tenth of that number: Colonel Kiyono Ichiki's detachment of 916 storm-troops at Truk got the call.

Like his boss, Ichiki was of the erroneous belief that he could make a landing on Guadalcanal and strike inland to the westward. By hitting swiftly, believed Ichiki, his forces could roll up the Marines and keep things under control until the arrival of Hyakutate's main body. The general, meanwhile, visited Admiral Mikawa's headquarters. It was nice that the IJN had redeemed itself for the debacle at Midway, Hyakutate opined. Now what assistance could the victorious Mikawa offer? The scourge of Savo listened patiently to the vain and haughty visitor, then calmly told him that there wasn't very much he could do. The admiral explained that American submarines were infesting the waters of the South Pacific, particularly around New Britain and New Ireland, and he wasn't about to lose another cruiser as he had lost *Kako* to a spread of *S-44*'s fish.

What he could do was this: provide escort for two transports for the Ichiki detachment in the form of cruiser *Jintsu* and destroyers *Hamakaze, Hagikaze, Arashi, Tanikaze,* and *Urakaze,* beyond which he could order Submarine Squadron 7 (*I-121, I-123, RO-33* and *RO-34*) to make savage attacks and shell the Guadalcanal beaches. Hyakutate agreed to the proposition. Any cooperation from the IJN, he reasoned, was better than none at all.

On Guadalcanal, the first amphibious Catalina moved off the airstrip on the 12th and five days later, Vandergrift radioed Ghormley that the strip was completely operational. Crude it was with a makeshift barracks, mess

54

nall and fuel tanks and—in addition—the Guadalcanal weather was abominable. However, the first Marine Corps fighters arrived on August 20 and everybody breathed a sigh of relief.

Vandergrift, at this point, was concentrating on his ground defenses. Nightly his forces were subjected to shelling from the sea, but the Marines came to regard this as routine and learned to adjust to the inconvenience. However, where it regarded the Japanese forces on Guadalcanal, Vandergrift wanted to know more. His patrols had penetrated to the Matanikau and found there, on August 10, an encampment of sorts and a number of Jap automatic weapons. Where, he pondered, was the main encampment?

A Marine Corps sergeant named Custer proposed to find out by taking a boat, landing on the west side of the river and thence probing inland. He was sure he'd find something—and he was right. In American hands at this time was a captured Jap naval rating, an irksome, argumentative little man who reluctantly admitted that the bulk of his countrymen were west of the Matanikau. This dovetailed with a report extant of a white flag seen in the vicinity.

Colonel Frank Goettge, 1st Division intelligence officer, hopped into the breach and, assuming the enemy was ready for surrender, decided on a landing whence he would take his patrol inland and find the enemy. He found the Jap all right, but there was no ready surrender. Instead, his patrol was wiped out, only three of 26 men escaping to impart this story to the Marine general. The so-called surrender flag was an army standard, meatball tucked neatly inside. When last seen by Goettge it was in the hands of some not very submissive Japs. Vandergrift's men cooled their tempers for a week, and on August 20 at Kokumbona and Matanikau beat down, with artillery and deadly rifle fire, enemy suicide waves in the number of 65 killed as opposed to 4 Marine casualties.

The following day on the eastern sector, Marines who'd thus far seen precious few Japs found them on the sandy banks of the Tenaru. These were Colonel Ichiki's men, primed and ready to go. Thirty-one of them walked into a Marine ambush in the first phase of this epic battle. Vandergrift's men dug into the left bank of the Tenaru and waited for the main body to materialize.

Mikawa's six destroyers now made their presence known, for in addition to landing the Ichiki Detachment safely, they bombarded the Tulagi docks with great gusto. Marines, behind their guns on the Tenaru, realized that it was only a matter of hours before this force would cross the river. Or try to.

Intelligence had pinpointed the coming of Ichiki's detachment (Major Martin Clemens of the Guadalcanal Defense Force and 60 natives) and, beyond this, there were the regular Marine intelligence estimates. So, then, the Marines waited and watched across the muddy waters for the little yellow men who were coming through the jungle.

At 1:30 A.M. the battle opened. Along a narrow sandbar barely 50 yards long, 200 bayonet-fixed Japanese raged across toward Marine positions, screaming and shouting in a classic *banzai* charge. Led by saber-waving officers, the Japanese troops stormed across the shallows into the teeth of rifle, machinegun and grenade fire—withering fire that cut down the officers and many of the men but did not eventually stop the charge from crossing the river. Marines fought bayonet to bayonet, knife to knife, smashing and hurling back the insanely shrieking Japanese.

Every enemy soldier who was caught on the left bank of the river at daylight was dead, and those who managed to crawl away hid in a coconut grove which, in the afternoon, first received smothering Marine fire and then a charge by Colonel Cresswell and his battalion. Here, behind fronds and hidden in palm trees, was the main body of Ichiki's force. By late afternoon, several additional determined bayonet charges were beaten off and the last Jap soldier was killed. The Marines counted their dead: 35, and 75 wounded.

Ichiki, found dead with a bullet in his brain, had burned his colors at the end of the battle. Fletcher Pratt, biographer of the Marine Corps, remarks that in the colonel's diary was found a neat schedule: "17 August. The landing. 20 August. The march by night and the battle. 21 August Enjoyment of the fruits of victory . . ."

Reported Lieutenant General Hyakutate to Tokyo: "The Ichiki Detachment was not successful."

The Tenaru was written into Marine Corps history as the first pitched engagement. It was a model of coordination and fire power and guts.

The Navy, meanwhile, was busy assisting in the Henderson Field operation. On August 20 the converted merchantman *Mormacmail,* now the jeep carrier *Long Island,* steamed in with two Marine Squadrons of Wildcats and Dauntless dive-bombers. On 24 August carrier *Enterprise* contributed her entire complement of dive-bombers. And by the end of the month still another air group, led by Colonel Wallace of the South Pacific Combat Air Transport, flew in.

Many were the pitched and oft-times lopsided battles of these few American aircraft against Zeros and Bettys. But the Marines held their own. They had to. Everything depended on an operational Henderson Field.

On 24 August, fifteen days after Savo, the storm which had been threatening since Mikawa's foray, broke with devastating fury in the lower Solomons.

The Japanese, since their stunning night victory, had amassed a force consisting of four carriers, two battle-ships, 12 cruisers, 20 destroyers, more than 15 transports, cargo ships and oilers, and 160 land-based bombing and fighter planes.

The *samurais* had gathered and, irked by United States Marine tenacity in holding Guadalcanal, decided to subject enemy American forces to a showdown at the end of the month with the commencement of Operation "KA." The plan called for Combined Fleet, Admiral Ksoroku Yamamoto commanding, to support a rein-forcement of 1,500 troops. Eighth Fleet (Outer South Seas Force) would harass the enemy with nightly shell-fire and 25th Air Flotilla would send down incessant flights.

Against Japanese forces the United States Navy mus-tered three carriers, one new battleship, five heavy cruisers, one light cruiser, and 15 destroyers—essen-tially the same task force built around Vice Admiral Frank Jack Fletcher's *Enterprise, Saratoga* and *Wasp* which had participated in the invasion. Fletcher, smart-ing from the Savo debacle, was now cruising with Task Force Fox in Solomons' waters looking for trouble.

The Japanese, coming down nightly in their "Tokyo Express," were plaguing American Marines. But the Navy decided against showing its hand in favor of wait-ing for the propitious moment—at all costs. *Blue* is a fair illustration of all costs.

With destroyers *Helm* and *Henley, Blue* was escorting supply ships *Alhena* and *Fomalhaut*. Steaming into Lengo Channel at about the time the Express was due to land supplies and men, the two cans were patrolling at 10 knots, radars alert. At 3:55 A.M. *Blue*, steaming eastward and 400 yards ahead of *Henley,* made a contact on sound and radar. Initial range was 5,000 yards. *Blue's* skipper ordered flank speed and brought torpedo tubes to bear at 3,000 yards. But a few moments before he did, alert Japanese eyes spotted the silhouette of an enemy vessel and down came the Long Lances.

By one minute to three, both ships had fires and the ones that came from the Orient arrived at their destination first. *Blue,* a solid sheet of flame about her fantail, lost 10 men killed and 21 wounded. The enemy destroyer was *Kawakaze,* whose cargo was now disembarked and whose course at 3 A.M. was northeast through The Slot at high speed.

Blue, because Intelligence reports said that the Japs were coming in force, was scuttled on orders from Rear Admiral Turner, who had returned from his unhappy retreat to the Fijis.

So far as the IJN was concerned, the Navy admitted nothing, and Task Force Fox remained in the shadows, waiting. Her exact position was about 150 miles east of Henderson Field. At 6:30 A.M. of the 23rd, 20 SBDs took off from *Enterprise* on a 200-mile arc drawn search, a slightly tense search because Fletcher was aware that the Jap was coming but he was unaware of his position and strength.

Yamamoto, with five groups built around Nagumo's Carrier Striking Force, was ready to present his calling card. His intention was to suck the enemy in by offering *Ryujo* as bait, and while U.S. carrier planes were in the process of attacking his small carrier, Nagumo's force of large carriers would then strike the American flattops and Henderson Field, meanwhile supporting a landing of 1,500 troops on Guadalcanal.

While the Japs were thus steaming toward Guadalcanal, one of Admiral John McCain's search planes flying from tender *Mackinac* sighted enemy transports.

Unlike the Hudsons in the Savo farce, this pilot promptly notified Commander Aircraft South Pacific and at 10:17 American commanders were notified that two cruisers and three destroyers covering transports, were making 17 knots for Guadalcanal: latitude 04° 40′ S., Long. 161° 15′ E. This put the enemy force only 281 miles from Fletcher's carrier groups!

A flurry of astonishment gripped Task Force Fox. Captain DeWitt Ramsey of the *Saratoga* ordered an immediate attack with 31 SBDs and 6 TBFs. (Ninety minutes later Guadalcanal Marines got into the act with a 23-plane strike. *Sara's* Air Group 3, incidentally, was led by Commander Harry D. Felt, present Commander-in-Chief of the Pacific Fleet.) These searches revealed nothing because of thickening weather and all aircraft came home that evening to an uneasy roost. By the following afternoon, Admiral Fletcher realized his long-sought engagement was just about at hand as reports of enemy task forces streamed into *Saratoga's* plot.

Fletcher immediately ordered another search, and this time the enemy force was found 225 miles distant! En route to plaster Henderson Field were *Ryujo's* aircraft and those of the 25th Air Flotilla from Rabaul, but these planes were successfully intercepted and the airstrip was only slightly damaged. Fletcher, roundly criticized for his famous pullback at Savo, now took the initiative.

Up went *Sara's* groups led by Felt, 29 bombers and seven torpedo planes finding the "bait" at 4:06. The weather was perfect, ceiling unlimited. This was the opportunity for which Felt had been waiting a long 24 hours, and his planes took full advantage of it. Diving from 14,000 feet as the enemy carrier and her screen went into tight circle maneuvers, Scouting Squadron 3 attacked first.

As American SBDs pounced on planes sent off *Ryujo*, Felt called in Bombing Squadron 3. Three 1,000-pound bombs landed smack on the carrier's deck, the planes attacking from the bow and stern so that either way a rudder change would expose the carrier to warheads. TBFs of Torpedo Squadron 8 attacked *Ryujo* last with torpedo releases held in check because of the heavily-smoking carrier until the last minute—drops were at 200 feet, ranges less than a half mile.

The enemy was caught with most of her aircraft gone. Her destroyer screen, also taking it, was no match for Felt's fury and it was all over by 5:20 when attack groups rendezvoused and streaked for home. They had left in their wake sinking tin cans and a flaming coffin, *Ryujo*—the bait which at 10 P.M. would roll over briefly, turn up her holed bottom and admit the sea in a gurgling death. There were a dozen air engagements between Felt's group and enemy planes, but at 6:46 when all planes touched down on *Sara*'s deck not a pilot or crewman was put on the Navy's casualty list. Yamamoto's bait had not proven so seductive after all.

Enterprise pilots had been busy this day too. When the radar screen revealed twenty-seven fighters, 36 dive bombers and 12 torpedo planes coming in fast, Big E pilots promptly took off. But of this large enemy formation only thirty-five dive dombers managed to penetrate. Screaming down on battleship *North Carolina* and *Enterprise* at 70° angles, the Jap waited until he was at 1,500 feet before releasing bombs.

The first bomb plummeted down and crashed into the carrier's flight-deck elevator aft, then mushed through the hangar deck into a third compartment. Thirty-five men dead.

The second bomb hit about 20 feet away and knocked out two 5-inch guns. Thirty-eight dead.

The third bomb hit abaft the island. No dead. But the three had turned the after end of the *Enterprise* into a holocaust with 95 wounded among the fatalities.

Jap losses also were heavy. A murderous flak thrown up by the ships of Task Force Fox repeatedly scored—considering the number of attacking planes and the size of the targets, more than three hits should have been registered. Destroyer *Grayson*, riding close aboard the carrier, alone accounted for a dozen; and an unnamed Negro steward's mate, a gun pointer, joyously observed: "Ah done got four of the bastards!"

Enterprise was licking her wounds, her Damage Control parties moving aft as remnants of the attacking force closed in on *North Carolina*. Yet despite her size and speed, the battleship poured out such a volume of concentrated 20-mm fire that no Jap actually saw his bombs hit paydirt before he went on to Imperial heaven. All bombs splashed harmlessly. The men who'd pressed the release buttons were Magumo's pride and joy, sent off to avenge the sinking of IJN carriers at Midway.

"Where were enemy torpedo planes during the battle, the vicious 'Kates' which had done for *Lexington* at Coral Sea and *Yorktown* at Midway?" Rear Admiral Morison asks. "*North Carolina* reported possible approaches of this type, but no other ship saw a torpedo plane or a torpedo. Wildcats claimed splashing four, but there were others unaccounted for. Some may have been operational casualties, but the rest must have been shot down by combat air patrol."

Within the hour, *Enterprise* was making 24 knots and ready to recover planes. All fires were out. Her ensign was spaking proudly in the late afternoon breeze as she moved away to rendezvous with fleet oilers *Cimarron* and *Platte* elsewhere in the South Pacific. A well-disciplined crew commanded by apta in Arthur A. Davis, thoroughly trained and alert, had pulled her through despite a jammed rudder which had nearly caused a collision with one of her screening destroyers.

Luck played its part in the battle—a decisive part perhaps. Admiral Nagumo's second strike had veered off course to the westward at the last minute, missing the flaming "Big E" when she was almost helpless, returning home after finding no targets. Then, too, there were the American TBFs who mistook a surf-lashed reef for high-speed warships and, because fuel was running dangerously low, had to jettison torpedoes and head for *Enterprise*.

This carrier, having effected repairs to the best of her ability, departed southward to link up with the *Wasp* group (which had seen no action) on the theory that the Jap was not quite finished yet, and it was better under the circumstances to have two air groups available in case of need. By now it was abundantly clear to Admiral Fletcher that the enemy's firepower was apparently much greater than his and he would do well to sheer clear. He did, leaving destroyer *Grayson* behind to sniff out American downed pilots.

Vice Admiral Nobutake Kondo, commanding the Guadalcanal Supporting Forces with a battleship (*Mutsu*) and a horde of cruisers and destroyers, still had a taste for battle. Eager to exploit the initiative—for his returning pilots had told him of extensive damage to at least one battleship and two carriers, Kondo ordered up full speed and charged toward Fletcher's last-known position. But darkness having descended on the waters of the Solomons and his planes finding only *Grayson*, Admiral Kondo, facing facts and not wishing to be caught in his own type of bear trap, disconsolately turned north and beat it clear of the area.

In the aftermath, perhaps the saddest of the Japanese commanders was Rear Admiral Raizo Tanaka, commander of the Transport Group. He had lost badly damaged light cruiser *Jintsu* to a Marine shavetail (Second Lieutenant Larry Baldinus) who planted a 500-pound bomb between his forward guns. This hit caused flooding to the magazines, slowing the cruiser to a crawl and leaving 61 casualties.

Tanaka, shifting his two-starred flag to destroyer *Kagero*, ordered smoke-shrouded *Jintsu* back to Truk. In this same melee transport *Kinryu Maru*, 9,300-tons, also took a direct hit. Dead in the water and crowded with troops, Tanaka quickly ordered destroyer *Mutsuki* to close and remove her survivors. Even as this was being done and the can hove to, over came a squadron of MacArthur's Flying Fortresses and down came a stick of bombs. *Mutsuki* caught it and promptly rolled over on her beam ends.

Tanaka at this time received orders to quit his run on Guadalcanal and head for the Shortlands. It was probably just as well that he did.

So ended the slam-bang phase of this battle, termed by Admiral Nimitz, Commander-in-Chief of the Pacific Fleet "a major victory which permitted consolidation of our positions in the Solomons."

In Washington, Admiral King was able now to say that "as a result of the action, the Japanese were all but stripped of carrier support and broke off the fight although their powerful surface forces were still largely intact."

And Frank Jack Fletcher, back again at his favorite resting place off San Cristobal where he was preparing to take the damaged Enterprise back to Pearl Harbor, again looked good. Some of the stigmata for Savo had disappeared with the excellent thinking—excellent bombing of Yamamoto's invasion force.

THE BUILDUP: PARRY AND THRUST

PROUD, HAUGHTY Lieutenant General Hyakutate could take a punch. Twenty-four hours after the Eastern Solomons route, he was back for more. On tap were 3,500 troops of the Kawaguchi Brigade, but instead of embarking them as a unit, he decided rightly to commit them piecemeal by way of the Tokyo Express. It was better, the general reasoned, to nibble away at Guadalcanal's Marines than to do no nibbling at all.

Accordingly 450 men were landed on the eastern flank, Taivu Point, after nightfall. Then, two nights later, Hyakutate sent down another element and this group was lucky too. In addition, the IJN retrieved a bit of face for the loss of *Asagiri*. A diversion strike by planes of the 25th Air Flotilla accounted for stripped-down destroyer *Calhoun*, now a fast transport. Bombers caught her at 3:12 P.M.

The American can, with sister ship *Little*, was screening auxiliary *Kopara* who was disgorging supplies. *Calhoun's* name was written on Jap bombs and there wasn't much she could do about it. Her lack of gunfire played a good part in her demise. As 18 planes popped out of the clouds above Guadalcanal, Lieutenant Commander G. B. Madden called for flank speed and radical maneuvering. Neither helped. Two Jap formations came in with their eggs for a wholly accurate, swift death. The foremast toppled, the 4-inch mounts were twisted off, all machinery and pipes were ripped from their moorings. Bombs literally blew the frantically maneuvering tin can apart in two minutes, and *Calhoun* dipped beneath the waves with a loss of 51 men. After the raid, tank lighters from Guadalcanal came out and fished up the rest of the crew. Jap destroyer *Yudachi* had no trouble landing her quota of Kawaguchis that night.

August was on its way out, but there was more grief in store for the Navy before the so-called September lull rolled around. Twenty-four hours after *Calhoun* dipped under a prowling Jap I-boat sneaked in through *Saratoga's* screen and pickled her. The carrier had just secured from morning General Quarters and all hands were on their way to chowdown, when *Sara* got it. At the precise moment that destroyer *MacDonough* made sound contact and saw a periscope 30 feet from her—even scraped it—*I-26* was getting off her fish. The tin can's quartermaster ran up the submarine warning signal and aboard *Saratoga,* Captain DeWitt Ramsey who saw it, spat out the order for full speed and tried twisting away. But the carrier wasn't fast enough to comb torpedo wakes.

The first and only fish that hit her, smashed in abaft the island, starboard side. A great geyser of oily water shot up, deluging stunned bluejackets and officers already racing to their Battle Stations, but by now—7:48 A.M.—*I-26* was long gone and heading for deep water. *MacDonough* and *Phelps* charged off in pursuit, a hunt which was joined later in the morning by *Monssen* who stuck to the contact area and plastered it with depth charges in a daylong hunt. *I-26,* headed for a long life, hit a good gradient and her savvy skipper promptly departed, his sub intact except for a few paint scratches. *Saratoga,* meanwhile, nursed her superficial bruises and her engineers patched up her electrical innards. By afternoon he was making a respectable 12 knots, with promise of more to come. A favorable wind and a tow by cruiser *Minneapolis* helped. But the skipper, understandably concerned with possible future attacks, ordered up his complement of aircraft and had them flown off to Espirutu Santo, about 350 miles distant. From there, they were sent to assist in the safeguarding of Guadalcanal.

I-26, while not actually making a kill, had achieved a very smart form of success: immobilization for several months of one of the Navy's most needed carriers . . .

On Guadalcanal, Vandergrift's people were getting some pretty odd reports. The regular schedule of the Tokyo Express was an unnerving piece of business, but no more so than scouts' reports of smoke rising from Savo Island. Were the Japs, in addition to Guadalcanal landings, getting ready for something new? Vandergrift wondered. Was Savo Island going to be the scene of another hot battle for his Marines?

Vandergrift took the bit in both jaws.

A marine detachment was quietly slipped onto the island at dark and closed on the spot where suspicious smoke had been seen. Around a fire, cooking chow, flabbergasted gyrenes found a handful of woolly-headed Melanesians. These natives, as much surprised as the fiercely armed men who found them, promised faithfully to do their cooking before noon henceforth ever on. And thus the issue was resolved. Vandergrift, reassured, turned back to the problems inherent in ferreting out the Kawaguchi Brigade.

"Everybody heaved a sigh of relief," said one officer in Vandergrift's operations setup. "The momory of what happened off Savo was bad enough, we didn't want any new business from that quarter . . "

Efforts to derail the Tokyo Express were largely unsuccessful, however. Usually coming down on the dark of the moon, and nights here were normally of 12 hour duration, Jap tincans had things pretty much their own way. But it was tricky business. The Express would form up and steam southward at full speed, unload, and turn around again for a return to base before dawn. The few American planes at Henderson Field, hampered by in

67

adequate radar and short-radius, usually came up dry. And after the Japs learned not to give themselves away with gunfire, there was no question about the success of their operation.

The sinking of the APDs *Little* and *Gregory* was one instance, however, where gunfire made the difference. Three Jap destroyers and a cruiser took the Guadal beaches under fire while unloading (*Hatsuyuki*, *Murakumo* and *Yudachi*, and *Yubari*) troops. This night American luck was running consistently bad, and it manifested itself in the form of a well-intentioned Catalina pilot who decided forthrightly to give the enemy a hard time. Like the men of the *Little* and *Gregory*, who thought the shooting emanated from a surfaced enemy submarine, so too did the pilot of the Cat. He immediately zoomed over the spot and dropped a string of five flares. At Savo, Mikawa's float jobs did the flare dropping, but here it was the case of the Helpful Cat. His flares starkly silhouetted the APDs and startled Jap gunners obliged by shifting targets. Instant death ensued.

Superior Jap night gunnery, overwhelming superiority in weapons, and speed made the difference. *Little* was hit in the engine rooms and steering was inhibited by a jammed rudder. The skipper, Lieutenant Commander G. B. Lofberg, decided to beach. His ship was a flaming pyre as shells screamed in and ignited the Higgins boats, smashed the steam line and deluged the bridge. Division Commander Hugh W. Hadley, riding the same bridge, was killed alongside Lofberg. Pretty much the same mess occurred aboard *Gregory*, except that the skipper was wounded in the initial melee. Taken over the side, he ordered his rescuers to leave him and to save a man who was drowning nearby. When the *Gregory* sailors charged to their lifesaving mission in compliance, that was the last seen of Lieutenant Com-

68

mander Harry F. Bauer. He had disappeared from his own liferaft when they swam back. Thirty-three killed, 70 wounded.

In Admiral Turner's report filed the following December 12, the commander of the transports speaks of the three APDs as follows:

". . . The officers and men serving in these ships have shown great courage and have performed outstanding service. They entered this dangerous area time after time, well knowing their ships stood little or no chance if they should be opposed by any surface or air force the enemy might send into those waters. On the occasion of their last trip in they remained six days, subjected to a daily air attack and anticipating nightly surface attack."

So it was. Stripped down to essentials, these former four pipers could only offer token resistance at best—a main battery of one gun and a few machineguns. Everything had been removed to accommodate Marines and their equipment . . .

The desperate struggle for Guadalcanal moved into September and while a third major battle was in the blueprint stage, the enemy sent down only planes and his Tokyo Express. A new element of naval warfare was introduced, however, when the discovery was made that the Jap was using barges to ferry in his troops. Small, interrelated wars sprang into life as the American 'spitkit' navy (PTs and the like) worked these troop-laden barges over along the close-ashore coastlines of the lower Solomons.

But it was during this period that the bulk of the 25th Air Flotilla met with stunning reverses. Each bomber strike, regardless of how well it was covered with fighters, was proving successively costly. Multi-gunned B-17s were taking on Jap fighters without thought of consequence and knocking them out of the skies. Even PBYs tangled with Kawanishis and usually came out on top.

For Vandergrift, there was a plus sign too: Colonel Merritt Edson, boss of the Raiders. This Marine officer and his men found plenty of small wars at Tasimboko, hacking up Kawaguchi's units with great dexterity—and this included blowing ammo dumps, knocking off field pieces and capturing a quartermaster's dump with all accoutrements.

"To be the recipient of these insulting attacks by American forces is maddening," the general scribbled in his diary, while others of his troops jotted similar comments. These men, out of some of the crack Jap armies around the world, had gone by the Imperial Staff Manual which declared that the enemy was gutless and would run in the face of the first counter-attack. The few survivors who got to a radio, proclaimed the Imperial Manual all wet. They knew.

On the sea off Guadalcanal, September brought a paradoxical situation to light. By night, enemy destroyers and cruisers ranged with impunity in these waters in unchallenged military superiority; by day American ships had freedom of movement here. Thus every twelve hours the waterways changed hands, and with it complete military superiority, but the Japs were beginning to gain an edge with the movement by barge of vast numbers of troops. Vandergrift, so concerned for his men that he called for a conference, wanted long-range bombers to wipe out the enemy.

Accordingly the Army Air Force represented by General George C. Kenney and the Army by General Sutherland, MacArthur's Chief of Staff, and the Navy by Nimitz, Ghormley and Turner met aboard Ghormley's flagship to settle the matter. The enemy, at this time, had covetous eyes for Port Moresby again despite the earlier thwarting in the Coral Sea and a leg-up approach from Tulagi shortly after. To further complicate matters, there existed strong inter-service rivalry and a politician's move to upgrade MacArthur as the real hero, the lonely sentinel. There was no question that the enemy was moving on Port Moresby via overland route, and MacArthur, rather than offer Fort coverage of the Guadal area, stuck to his contention that the Pacific Fleet should help his forces instead of being concerned about Jap troop movements. This tended to strengthen the bridge between Army and Navy.

Undersecretary of the Navy James Forrestal was asked by Navy sources to come down and view the situation first-hand. He did. Then he returned to Washington and, visibly angered by what he had seen, urged that Ghormley, Turner and Vandergrift receive reinforcements. This they received, but there was no assistance from MacArthur forthcoming. With the Japs only 32 miles from Port Moresby, he had his hands full before he finally stopped their overland advance.

For the Navy, these were days of parry and thrust with nothing as substantial as battle on the horizon. But for the Marines, these were the black days when Vandergrift fully anticipated a large scale attack from at least 4,000 enemy troops on the island. The general's list of grievances against the Army and Navy was growing in inverse proportion to his own dwindling aircraft and human casualties. He was justly alarmed. The biographer of the Marine Corps, Fletcher Pratt, summed up the gyrene's plight:

"What was needed was a good big convoy with reinforcements and everything else implied in that word. General Vandergrift kept the communications channels hot asking for it—but most especially for planes, at once."

General Kawaguchi, Vandergrift's opposite number, was a typical product of the book-prone Imperial system. Even after the debacle at Tasimboko where his first contingent met its fate trying to "Remember the Ichiki Detachment!" the general insisted that he would

71

make his decisive engagement in the Tasimboko area.

Vandergrift, feeling the first fine drizzle of the approaching storm, strengthened the eastern flank of the Tenaru as one of the likely places of possible attack. At the termination of the river was an irregularly-shaped ridge where his Raiders had established themselves in foxholes. The Pioneer Battalion was holding down a strongpoint to the rear down to the Lunga River. Grassy Knoll, dominating the landscape, was uncovered. If the Japs hit here, Vandergrift would be obliged to call in divisional reserves. The 7th Marine Regiment which had been garrisoned at Samoa, now was aboard transports and moving to Guadalcanal, the result, no doubt, of Vandergrift's small voice in the recent parlay.

But there were no reserves on hand for the night of September 12. At nine o'clock, Vandergrift's fears were realized. A green flare suddenly exploded over Henderson Field and in the same moment shells began to scream over from the sea. Here were three destroyers and a cruiser with orders to shell regardless of where the fireballs dropped. Kawaguchi's men were all over the place. Shouting and yelling insanely, they ripped up Edson's line in a rush of mortar fire, nipped the communications line and isolated a company at the western end of the ridge. When Edson recovered from the onslaught, the Japs were securely dug in and there were so many of them that Edson sagely withdrew to the north end of the ridge.

An observer, Twining, reported the precarious position of the Raiders to Vandergrift. The Marines had been on their feet throughout all the hard fighting of the campaign. They were walking dead, pushed to their limit of endurance and talking to themselves. The Jap rockets kept coming and so did fresh attacks, one of the last pushing Captain John B. Sweeney's men to a position within 1,500 yards of the airfield. Their screaming charges were punctuated with cries of *"Roosevelt die! Marine pig! Gas attack now! Babe Ruth eat s—!"* The demoniacal fury of their bayonet charges against a curtain of American fire (howitzers, machineguns, mortars, rifles and grenades) ended in death for most, while survivors were hauled off into the jungles before daylight. On the following night Kawanguchi's men tried the same stunt again only from different hotspots on the line, but the line held again and in the morning there were more bloody corpses on Edson's Ridge and the ridge south of Kukum.

Marines dead: 40, and 103 wounded. Kawanguchi dead: about 1750. The battle of the Marines at Edson's Ridge was one of the key actions of the campaign. Few engagements would be harder fought, or for a more important cause. By holding off Jap hordes from Henderson Field, the Marines had held the damnable island and probably shortened the war. Vandergrift could be proud. Marine skill and courage had won out.

The Navy, meanwhile, was keeping busy. Out from Espirutu Santo sailed the 7th Marine Regiment in convoy. Vice Admiral Ghormley now committed his two operational carriers *Hornet* and *Wasp* in a task force built around them. While Marines were burying their dead on Guadalcanal, this task force was keeping well to the westward by day to prevent the enemy from gaining knowledge of the convoy. The two carriers launched air searches, resulting in a conglomeration of reports all indicating the same thing—plenty of Jap warship movement to the north.

Movement of this all important convoy (the only Marine replacement in the South Pacific was the 7th) was effected by keeping the transports heading into Guadalcanal while the carriers remained far to sea. Admiral Turner had to get his troops ashore somehow and sailing steadily for the island was risky business. Around mid-morning of the 15th the transports were snooped by a Jap flying boat, but Turner maintained course, although it was his intention to turn away at the coming of nightfall. Still, despite the beauty of the day at sea, there was deep apprehension. Would Turner get his Marines landed? This was the cliffhanger. For where there had been a normal amount of tension before, there was now—since the sighting of an enemy flying boat— only ominous silence and grave looks. It was a morning to be remembered . . .

The sea was yellow with sunlight, freshened by a brisk 20-knot wind. Cruisers and destroyers milled around *Wasp*, six miles distant from *Hornet* who was surrounded by her own screen including the battleship *North Carolina*, cruisers, and destroyers. On flight decks, planes stood manned and ready, gassed and waiting for a takeoff order. But despite the sighting of the enemy flying boat and the attendant tension, nothing much happened until early afternoon—then it happened all at once.

At 2:20 P.M. *Wasp*, flying the two-starred flag of Rear Admiral Leigh Noyes, the carrier responsible for the day's combat air and anti-submarine patrol, turned into the wind to launch and recover planes. Twenty-six SBDs and Wildcats roared off her flight deck on signal; 11 combat air patrol planes returned. This launching was still in progress as *I-19*'s skipper furtively lifted her periscope and gazed in ecstatic amazement at the big prize— an American carrier, her decks heavy with planes!

The enemy submarine commander closed in for a better look. None of the six destroyers milling around the flattop had detected him on their sonar gear. The Jap tersely whispered the order to open outer torpedo doors and stand by. His setup was perfect. As the last of the planes to be launched flew off *Wasp*'s deck, Captain Forrest Sherman gave the order for right rudder to return her on base course. The Japanese submariner had meanwhile snapped out the order for six fish forward, and the fish were away. Then from high atop the bridge came the cry:

"Torpedoes! Torpedoes starboard bow!"

It was too late. The first pair of Long Lances sundered in forward on the starboard side, the second pair broached but returned to track and hit forward of the bridge starboard side, and two fish raced under the destroyer *Lansdowne* to give that warship a bad scare. Aboard the flattop all hell broke loose.

On the flight deck, planes lifted off vertically and, crashing back to deck, smashed their landing gear. In the 'mystic maze,' gasoline fires, spreading from the hangar deck, ignited in the vacuous compartment and sent tongues of flame racing toward the wardroom. In the hangar deck, planes suspended from the overhead, being worked on by the ship's mechanics, plummeted to the deck and shattered atop the sailors there. In the engineroom, main propulsion was somehow maintained after a shifting of fuel tanks—low side to high side—by an alert petty officer. But here switchboard panels and generators twisted off their moorings, and the machinery foundered in a deluge of fuel oil. On deck, ready ammo and bombs exploded and sent shrouding smoke up to the wheelhouse, while concussion of the explosions scythed down the living. Decks pitched over hard as the ship took a heavy starboard list. The island, smothered in smoke, was lacerated by shrapnel.

On the open bridge, Captain Forrest Sherman was standing beside the body of a young officer who had been blown from a turret. He was calmly conning the great flaming wreck, trying to put the light wind on his starboard quarter in an attempt to blow the fire away from the undamaged portions of the ship. Using small amounts of right and left rudder, Sherman was succeeding when he rang up 'stop' on the telegraphs. The engine-rooms complied. In the water were literally dozens of men strung out in the white-capped sea and Sherman, a man who was always concerned for his crew, had no intention of steaming away.

He had voice communication with his enginerooms and he had a crackerjack fire fighting team. This combination gave the captain of the *Wasp* a fair chance, but even the greatest of fire fighters was no match for this inferno. Captain Bill Chambliss was in the flag plot of the carrier.

"Here," he said, "I did not hear the warning shout at the approach of torpedoes. My first knowledge of something amiss came when I realized that the chart board and I were some feet above the deck. When I came down again, amid the scattered mess of chairs, navigational instruments and the interphone talker, I was thrown to my knees by a second and third violent shock as the last two torpedoes hit us. Smoke poured into the flag plot . . ."

Sherman, moving to the port wingtip, paid scant attention to the raging fires. "In the face of death," Chambliss recorded, "he was absolutely calm and we all remembered that . . ."

The inspiring spectacle of the flaming carrier was observed over the waters by an enemy submariner, the companion skipper of the *I-19*. He was some miles distant in *I-15*, closer aboard the *Hornet*'s group. Two in one day? He snapped out his Long Lances and watched them run down the track. Two destroyers twisted out of the way at the last second, but the battleship—the second choice in targets—erupted a tremendous spout of flame and water. A hole 32 x 18 appeared below the waterline, five men were killed instantly and a long-tongued flame spewed into the No. 1 handling room, but a flooding of the magazines here ended the Roman candle.

At 25 knots, *North Carolina* promptly quit the arena.

Destroyer *O'Brien* was not so lucky. A torpedo took her from keel to hawsepipe and knocked her bow off. The explosion, however, threw no pattern of consuming flame to shout out her death knell. Bow off and alert crew dogging down bulkheads, she shuddered like a rat in a terrier's jaws and stumbled forward at half speed.

But the day's big score for the pigboats of Japan's Submarine Squadron 7 was *Wasp.* A long afternoon of fire fighting had amounted to an enemy sinking—the carrier was doomed. About 3 P.M. flames became uncontrollable and spread to hitherto undamaged areas of the big carrier. This was the moment that a violent explosion rattled the entire ship. On the port side of the bridge, several men were instantly killed. Admiral Noyes, thrown to the signal bridge deck, was badly singed. Now it was decided to fight the battle of saving the carrier from Batt II, the after control, but as Noyes and his officers were about to quit the bridge another explosion heaved up the No. 2 flightdeck elevator and sent it crashing back on twisted wreckage. Still another explosion gutted the ship. Then forward the fire mains quit.

Sherman turned to Noyes. Words were unnecessary somehow. *Wasp* was finished. The admiral reluctantly gave the Abandon Ship order at 3:20 P.M. Men went over the side in orderly fashion, among them Admiral Noyes. When picked up by the *Fahrenholt,* one of the escorting destroyers, he directed Rear Admiral Norman Scott in *San Francisco* to take command. Then, because *Wasp* was tearing herself apart in monstrous fashion but not actually sinking, Scott gave destroyer *Lansdowne* the dreaded order: go in and sink.

The tincan complied with five fish and at 9 P.M., more than seven hours from the time that *I-19* fired her torpedoes, the gallant carrier died. Of the 2,247 men aboard, 193 were killed, 366 were wounded.

"The older people held out better than the young

ones," Chambliss recollected. "We had no boats and only five or six rafts on which to place our wounded. Crowding onto the rafts with the wounded were a number of young fellows. After we had been in the water for about two hours or so it was they who began to grunt and groan about the fact that we probably wouldn't be picked up . . ."

But they were.

In the *North Carolina* group, the battleship and the tincan *O'Brien* were detached. The wagon made it to Espirutu and Pearl Harbor with two escorts; the can made it alone. That is, she made it as far as Samoa where a beam let go and she broke into two even parts and sank. Turner's transports with the vital replacements, ammo and vehicles reached Guadalcanal: by their very presence in these waters, the carrier groups had discouraged a mass Japanese naval attack. But the price was prohibitive: a can, a carrier and a wagon out of the running, two of them permanently.

PART III

Cape Esperance

CRUISER DIVISION 6 of the Imperial Japanese Navy was looking for trouble. Not since the night of August 9 in Ironbottom Sound had there been a substantial victory. The small, sniping affairs around Guadalcanal were not alone costly but Imperial forces were really getting nowhere in their efforts to oust the Americans. Something decisive was needed.

In Rabaul, the cocky little commander of the Outer South Seas Force planned a daring operation. Mikawa, conferring with frustrated staff officers and equally frustrated Lieutenant General Hyakutate (he now planned to send down 25,000 reinforcements), conceived a big punch-naval engagement which was certain to wrest control of the Solomons. Admiral Yamamoto desperately wanted such a victory, for it was becoming increasingly difficult for him to explain the state of things to Emperor Hirohito.

On the other side of the coin, General Vandergrift had received Colonel Chesty Puller's 7th with open arms. Puller's men were now in the field up to their eyeballs in jungle fighting. New replacements were needed and Vice Admiral Ghormley, a good provider, came up with a solution—the 164th Infantry Regiment of the Americal Division stationed in New Caledonia. On October 9 transports lifting this outfit departed Noumea, on a course to pass north of San Cristobal. The debarking was scheduled for the 13th.

Ghormley, astutely figuring the Japs would be waiting with at least submarines to welcome the Americans at Lunga Point, planned to give the transports adequate cover.

For this operation, three groups were assembled: Rear Admiral Norman Scott's cruisers, Rear Admiral Willis A. Lee's built around Battleship *Washington* and Rear Admiral George Murray's built around *Hornet*.

Scott's outfit was chosen as an immediate "blocker" for the transports which were lifting 2,800 men, with an escort of eight destroyer-type screening ships. His two-starred flag was aboard cruiser San Francisco, and his orders from Ghormley read: "Search and destroy enemy ships and landing craft."

Tough, wiry Norman Scott welcomed the opportunity. One of the few naval commanders to have carefully drawn a battle plan thus far in the Pacific war, Scott had rehearsed his crews for a night action. They were primed and ready to go. The admiral at Savo had missed the gunplay by a whisker, but it wasn't his intention to miss again. For two days after arriving at his destination, the admiral's group, Task Force 64, steamed up and down the shores of western Guadalcanal waiting for word that the enemy was coming down in force. At 1:45 P.M., October 11, the bell signifying the opening round of the battle of Cape Esperance, sounded loud and clear: search planes from Guadalcanal had sighted what looked like a force of two enemy cruisers and six destroyers moving down The Slot at high speed.

"We will intercept," flashed the word by blinker. "All ships prepare for action."

The enemy force, 210 miles distant, was headed on a course that would put the action again in Savo Sound.

Task Force 64 sucked in its collective breath and waited.

At Rabaul, Captain Toshikazau Ohmae, planner of the Savo operation, also waited. For weeks, Ohmae had been under tremendous pressure from the Army to get troops to Guadalcanal, for another Savo would heap further disgrace on the enemy. Ohmae planned a joint operation with the Army, the purpose of which was to bring replacements to Guadal while a Navy task force attacked American surface forces, simultaneously bombarding Henderson Field. Should this new plan meet with success, likely it would mean the end of the Americans in the islands. This was the basic motivation and plan of the Japanese movement south.

The prelude to battle was a series of strikes and counter-strikes by the air arms of both countries. Fliers from Henderson Field had plastered Rabaul in a daylight and daylong series of attacks. Mikawa, Ohmae's superior, was in a stew. He went to see Vice Admiral Kusaka, commander of the Eleventh Air Fleet, to ask him to do something about the Americans from Henderson Field. Kusaka agreed if Mikawa would operate the Tokyo Express on the 11th, thus further removing the heat from the IJN insofar as General Hyakutake was concerned. That worthy, incidentally, was already on Guadal, having come down in the Express a couple of nights previously.

True to his assurances, Kusaka sent down 65 fighters and bombers on the 11th while Mikawa launched a force consisting of Savo veterans *Aoba*, *Kinugasa*, *Furutaka*, two destroyers and a reinforcement group of two seaplane carriers, *Chotise* and *Nisshin*. In command of the Japanese warships was Rear Admiral Arimoto Goto, a Mikawa disciple in the art of night attack.

At 10 P.M. Task Force 64 was prowling the waters off Cape Esperance, the northernmost tip of Guadalcanal. Readiness reports had streamed into Rear Admiral

Scott's battle plot from every ship in the force. There was nothing to do now but wait for Goto and hope that he maintained course.

San Francisco, in the lead, was followed by *Boise, Helena* and *Salt Lake City.* Destroyers *Laffey* and *Duncan* rode to starboard, *Fahrenholt* ahead, and *Buchanan* and *McCalla* to port, all escorts steaming in a half semi-circle awaiting word from Scott to assume final battle disposition.

As six bells struck in pilot houses, the admiral ordered up one float plane from each of his cruisers. *Salt Lake City's* OS2U, one of the first to be catapulted, crashed on takeoff and burned briskly for about four minutes before sinking. The crew of the plane inflated a raft and were directed toward Gudalcanal. Then Scott, a veteran of the World War I sea fighting, calmly took to pacing his bridge and waiting reports. He knew they would come soon enough.

The admiral, in 1917, had been executive officer of the destroyer *Jacob Jones.* He had been aboard when that vessel became the victim of a German U-boat in the Atlantic. Long years of shipboard life, staff work and more staff work had intervened between his first sinking and the combat of this night, but he was fully prepared, physically and mentally. A graduate of the Naval Academy Class of 1911, Norman Scott was a man of action. In the office of the Chief of Naval Operations in 1941, "he made life so unbearable for everybody around him that he was finally transferred to sea duty—what he wanted," Admiral Raymond A. Spruance said of him later.

At 10:28 P.M., with his float planes flying, this plesant-faced flag officer ordered a slight change of course and battle formation with 'Frisco still leading. The burning plane incident had drawn nerves tightly and sailors on all the ships wondered if this inordinate light would give them away. It did not. Scott, hoping to intercept off

Savo Island, still found the night "black as spades, punctuated with occasional flashes of lightning." The sea was calm. Then, at 10:52, the first of a series of sighting reports came up to the admiral:

"ONE LARGE AND TWO SMALL VESSELS X WILL INVESTIGATE X"

Scott was delighted. He assumed there were two formations, the cruisers and destroyers bringing up the rear.

Goto, rushing headlong into disaster with his force in T formation—cruisers in line, destroyers on flanks—saw something burning on the water and, after a moment of suspicion, discarded all thought of an enemy trap. He was making 26 knots and remaining on course for Guadalcanal—Savo in reverse! There was no question in his mind that he would get to Henderson Field and bombard, while covering the landings.

At 11:25 P.M., cruiser *Helena* who sported the new SG radar reported a contact "bearing 315 degrees, 27,000 yards distant." The "pip" soon became three, slowed now to 20 knots. But the first that Scott knew of this was fifteen minutes later when his search plane reported again. Curiously, his flagship wasn't equipped with SG. The enemy force was plotted and the order went out to stand by for main battery. Then *Boise* reported five pips.

Task Force 64 caught its breath.

On the *Boise*, first ship to open fire, Captain Mike Moran was standing in the center of the flying bridge, squinting into the blackness straight ahead. On his right was Commander William C. Butler, assistant gunnery officer, wearing a phone headset under his helmet. High above the bridge and just abaft it was Sam Forter, a young lieutenant, "a kid with dark hair, brushed straight back, and narrow piercing eyes." As director officer, Forter—a native of Boise, Idaho—held a key post. His job was to locate targets and set in motion the complicated machinery that would establish the direction and distance of those targets. Forter knew his business.

"On target!" snapped the word from Forter.

"How many ships?" Iron Mike shot back a split-second later as Guns relayed the question.

"Seems to be five, sir."

"Pick out the biggest and commence firing!"

And 15 guns fired in swift compliance with the order.

Then breeches flew open, the next shells were out of the hoists and rammed home with beautiful precision. Again the turrets shook.

In *Helena*, *Salt Lake City* and *San Francisco* the same situation was being repeated. *Helena's* first salvo drew blood, her 8-inch shells suddenly raining down on the unsuspecting Goto in much the same manner as at Savo. *Salt Lake City* took on a cruiser 4,000 yards off her starboard bow and had the satisfaction of seeing her shells rip into the warship at almost point-blank range. A moment later, the enemy snapped out of his lethargy and answered with fire of his own which killed several men aboard the cruiser. Admiral Scott's *San Francisco* debated the issue with a cruiser at 4,800 yards. The cans whammed away at anything, big or small.

Boise's 6-inch fire scored on the first round. An enemy cruiser burst into flame amidships, an inspiration for her happy gunners to pour out four minutes of withering fire until that vessel broke in two and sank, a pall of smoke hanging over the spot like a wreath.

"At first we thought the fire was from our own supply ships," said Captain Kikunori Kijuma, Goto's chief of staff aboard *Aoba*. "It was a surprise attack. All ships but the *Kinugasa* immediately reversed course to the right. Due to shellfire and the congestion, the *Kinugasa* turned left. As a result of this turn, she received only minor damage from three hits.

"The *Aoba* was hit about 40 times and was badly damaged. The *Furutaka* and *Fubuki* were sunk. *Murakumo* was not hit . . ."

In American destroyer ranks, hell busted loose. *Fahrenholt* was the victim of friendly fire. *Duncan,* finding herself between salvos, moved out and was almost clear when an enemy shell smashed into her No. 1 fireroom. *Laffey,* a sturdy contributor to *Aoba*'s plight, was also caught between fires, but successfully fell astern of *Helena*.

On the bridge of the Japanese flagship, Admiral Goto fell mortally wounded under the tidal wave of enemy shells. While he was dying, *Aoba*'s skipper was heard telling him he could depart happily inasmuch as the flagship's guns had sunk two enemy heavies. Hardly so.

On *San Francisco,* Admiral Scott was an interested but poorly informed commander of the winning team. Plagued by lagging communications and radar troubles, Scott kept looking in bewilderment at the milling silhouettes of many ships. In the sincere belief that his force was firing on friendlies, he suddenly gave the order to cease firing. It was 11:47, or just about one minute after the first American salvo. Many of Scott's ships disregarded the order at first and kept firing. Even *San Francisco*'s main batteries were pounding away at the enemy so that the admiral had to personally visit her bridge in order to insure compliance.

Even so, nothing could save the Japs this night. *Aoba* and *Furutaka* were blazing brightly in their own fires, and these bright sentinels of doom heralded an unprecedented defeat for the IJN. All through the Guadalcanal campaign, the IJN had held its own. More than held it, in fact, when considered in the light of Savo and the earlier campaigns in the Pacific and Indian Oceans.

The communications jinx, which didn't affect the outcome of the battle one way or the other, nevertheless gave the enemy a four-minute breather from American fire. The snafu had its beginnings when *Helena*'s skipper misinterpreted Admiral Scott's reply to his question requesting permission to fire. Scott had answered "Roger!" and *Helena*'s skipper construed the Roger to mean afirmative. Instead, the admiral had meant he understood the question. No matter . . . American luck was running high this night.

What really precipitated Scott's "Cease firing!" order was a report from destroyer Squadron Commander Tobin that his three cans were coming up to starboard. Scott was unable to distinguish these ships, besides which the black waters off Cape Esperance were boiling with other warships. He called Tobin on TBS: "How are you?" Tobin answered that he was all right. The admiral then said: "Well, I don't know who you were firing at." At nine minutes before midnight Tobin, acting on Scott's order to fire green identification flares, did so. Then the flagship's radio sputtered again: "Resume Firing!"

The breather didn't mean much to the punchdrunk Imperial Japanese Navy. Goto was breathing his last and so were many of his top commanders. Captain Kikunori Kijuma of *Aoba*, hearing reports that all his turrets and torpedo tubes had been put out of commission, saw the futility of remaining to absorb further punishment. He ordered the helmsman to put the wheel hard over and come about. The pilothouse, a shambles of flaming debris from 8-inch hits, was strewn with the dead and dying. *Aoba*'s skipper himself had been hit by shrapnel but rather than relinquish command, Kijuma snapped out the word to commence firing. Heavy cruiser *Furutaka* and destroyer *Hatsuyuki* turned the wrong way, but the remainder of his ships didn't. In this moment, the first Japanese shells screamed down on scrappy *Duncan*.

Despite the hit in her fireroom and another on her gun director, Lieutenant Commander E .B. Taylor slugged back. He was still conning to get clear of the area when his torpedo officer Lieutenant (jg) Robert L. Fowler fired a fish. The target was *Furutaka*. Simultaneously, Captain Kijuma's shells were coming down and one of them smashed into her forward stack, toppling it, while another turned the No. 2 handling room into an exploding abbatoir.

Fowler, mortally wounded, passed along his torpedo shooting chores to the chief torpedoman who fired a second fish. On deck, destroyer sailors were slamming out 5-inch at a silhouetted destroyer, probably *Murakumo*, which had great effect and slowed the onward rush of the enemy tincan. But Taylor, acutely aware of his predicament, was still very much a witness to the arrival of both friendly and enemy shells. He snapped on his recognition lights even as the vessel was shearing off at high speed. Too late. Salvos creamed the destroyer for fair from the direction of her own task force. She was out of action, her lights shot away, and mortally wounded.

Lieutenant Commander E. T. Seward's *Fahrenholt*, hit about the same time as *Duncan*, was another victim of American shells. In the initial moments of the battle, a shot ripped through the thin-skinned hull, flooded her gun plot and wrecked her fire control wiring. Another, equally costly, smashed into her No. 1 boiler, releasing a jet of murderous steam. Seward urged his Black Gang to hold out as long as possible, to which his water tenders replied: "Don't worry, Captain, we'll sail this bucket into Tokyo yet—"

Gallant retort notwithstanding, *Fahrenholt*'s crew just managed to clear the area, as a cross-connected engineering plant gave the destroyer steady pressure on her No. 2 boiler. But she was out of action and looked it, a heavy list on her starboard side which her crew vainly attempted to correct by shifting fuel and water. It was barely enough to carry her out of danger.

Aboard *San Francisco*, Captain McMorris' curiosity was

piqued by the silhouette of a strange ship flashing unintelligible signals on a yardarm blinker. This vessel was about a mile off his starboard bow. Whose ship was this? Then, as the silhouette fanned into light, McMorris saw the pagodas and white-circled funnel of the enemy. Simultaneously, Scott's "Resume Firing!" order came down and 'Frisco led the avalanche of main batter that poured into the victim, IJN *Fubuki*. At 1:53 the enemy tincan stopped dead, exploded, and sank.

Admiral Scott ordered his column of ships to come about and give chase in a northwesterly direction. *Boise*, on the turn, picked up a pip on her radar. "Light the bastard!" Iron Mike growled, and signalmen snapped on the cruiser's searchlights. For gunners aboard *Kinugasa* and *Aoba* who, up to now, had been the recipients of American punishment, the invitation was too good to be turned down. Frank Morris, biographer of the immortal Moran and Co. described the event:

"About this time the signal bridge reported splashes on both port and starboard sides, close aboard. These were salvos from an enemy heavy cruiser some distance ahead on *Boise*'s starboard bow. And as Mike Moran's men fired on her, the Jap cruiser returned the fire with gusto. Splashes from her salvos came nearer and nearer, throwing salt water over the *Boise*'s decks, superstructure, and anti-aircraft guns.

"Finally one of these shells (seven in all), an eight-incher, smacked into her starboard side, forward, just above the waterline. It exploded in the crew's mess hall. Two lighter shells, probably five-inch, hit the starboard side of the superstructure, and another pair pierced the side of the ship and let go in the Captain's cabin, wrecking the interior and setting it afire. 'Tell the gentleman I'm sorry I wasn't home,' Iron Mike murmured when news of what had happened to his cabin was relayed to him.

"Topside, *Boise*'s deck gunners were bearing the brunt of the enemy's return fire. Gun Captain King and his entire crew were hurled to the deck when No. 1 gun, the first five-inch gun on the starboard side, was struck by a Jap shell and put out of action. Shell fragments and hot empty shell cases from their own expended ammunition showered around them as they struggled to their feet. Joe Vignali, a 'hot-case' man, had just yanked one of these empty powder cartridges from the gun when the explosion knocked the case out of his hand. It bounced up, struck the overhead, and started to fall back. Vignali was an agile cuss—although he had been knocked down by the same hit, he was up on his knees in an instant and actually caught the hot case in his arms as it descended. 'Never dropped one yet,' he yelled above the din. 'Ain't about to start now!'

"Another member of the gun crew, First Class Seaman Pitzer, wasn't so lucky. A large shell fragment struck his knee, mangling it badly. When he tried to get up, he found he couldn't and he subsequently was carried off to a battle dressing station.

"Sightsetter Lowry, on No. 3 near-by, felt a sharp spray against his leg but he stuck to his post during the remainder of the action. After he finally collapsed and was carried off, one of the *Boise's* doctors dug thirty-two pieces of shell out of his leg and showed him the tin hat he had been wearing. In it was a jagged hole two inches across—a souvenir of that shell blast.

"Mike Moran's men had been so occupied in their job of Jap ships that it hadn't occurred to them that the *Boise* herself might be hit. One of them, a chief named Schermerhorn who acted as trainer on Sam Forter's director, was surprised and indignant when the barrage of Jap shells found their mark. 'What the hell!' he bellowed. 'The sons of bitches are shooting back at us!' "

Boise, listing and afire, skidded out of formation.

Salt Lake City was engaging an enemy cruiser when she saw Moran's pugnacious warship aflame. Immediately she shifted targets and silenced one of the ships that was giving *Boise* a hard time. It was 12 minutes after the hour of midnight. Captain Ernest G. Small had pulled a neat, and somewhat foolhardy trick. By placing his own vessel between American forces and the Japs, he was actually screening *Boise* while exposing *Salt Lake City* to enemy fire. But a magician is as good as his performance, and Small was just great in the first hour of October 12.

Admiral Scott's flagship acquitted herself well in the fight. Tangling with a cruiser at 7,000 yards, *San Francisco* was a leader of the gang that jumped *Kinugasa* and *Aoba*, pumping some 40 shells into the last named. *Salt Lake City*, protecting *Boise*, took two hits in her fireroom but was not otherwise slowed down. At 12:16 *McCalla* tangled with her own weight in an IJN tinclad and at 12:17 *San Francisco* fired her last salvo at a cruiser. The cruiser's pip disappeared from the radar screen and the destroyer barreled out wreathed in flames.

Time: 12:20 A.M. Silence at Cape Esperance. A signal 30 minute naval battle was over. Admiral Scott now attempted to collect his flock. Voice calls from *San Francisco* to *Duncan, Fahrenholt* and *Boise* were not acknowledged. Scott ordered *McCalla* to stand by to render necessary assistance. Then Scott's voice crackled over the airwaves:

"Standby for further action. This show may not be over yet."

But it was. Forty minutes later, the task force was homeward bound. *Boise*, flames roaring up from her damaged bow carried 107 dead, 35 wounded. Clipping along under her own power, she fell in astern of the flagship like a battered alley cat home from a night's campaign, tired, footsore and proud. She'd sunk ships. *Fah-*

renholt, injured in the opening round of the battle, received an assist from destroyer *Aaron Ward*, but was making it without tow lines. Of all the United States vessels present, only *Duncan* was *in extremis*. When she'd staggered out of battle, her bridge was a shambles, her forecastle warped and blazing. Everything of importance —radio shack, gun director platform, plot—was wrecked and burning. Her dead were everywhere. Wounded men crawled through smoke-filled passageways as blindly as their destroyer, circling like a dying fish at 15 knots.

Fires raged on the wings, the intense heat sending trapped lookouts and signalmen over the side to save themselves. The skipper, Commander Taylor, ordered the bridge abandoned but this was academic—most of her bridge crew had already departed. The wounded were lowered into rafts first, then the skipper and the uninjured leaped into the sea. However, unbeknownst to Taylor, there were still living crewmen below decks— men who believed that the bridge was abandoned and only dead were up above. One of them, Lieutenant H. R. Kabat, the engineering officer, heard the voice of Ensign Frank A. Andrews over the phone from after control. As senior officer, the engineer ordered Andrews to steer the destroyer toward the beach in order to ground her. Despite the titanic efforts of her crew, however, it was impossible to keep the boilers going and the vessel gradually lost power and stopped. Finally, the ammunition began to explode and there was nothing anybody could do but save himself. Sailors and officers jumped overboard, clinging to powder cases, rubbish, any flotsam that would keep them afloat until rescue. And so the fiery ship and the men drifted apart, the former eventually to be spotted by fellow tinclad *McCalla*, the latter to fall victim of savage attacks by a school of sharks. Thus things stood when *McCalla* closed the exploding wreck and her CO, Lieutenant Commander Cooper, sent a whaleboat over to determine whether the derelict could be saved.

The screams of the men in the water fortunately attracted the *McCalla*'s whaleboat, and rifle fire eventually peppered into the sharks and drove them away. But 48 crewmen went down with the *Duncan* at 11:30 the next morning. Her grave was six miles north of Savo Island.

For Captain Kijimi, senior officer of the Japanese task force, the retirement northward at high speed was a shameful and apprehensive business. His admiral was dead, his surviving ships shot through, and his Navy's dream of repeating the stunning Savo defeat on the enemy dissolved in a welter of smoke and fiery steel. Kijimi, fearing an aircraft strike as he raced up The Slot, dreaded the new day. His fears were realized. At 7 A.M., McCain's bombers found his thoroughly mauled ships and dropped sticks of bombs, but none hit and Kijimi and his ships arrived intact in the Shortlands. Only destroyers *Furutaka* and *Fubuki* had been lost in the melee. Destroyer *Murakumo* of the group of ships landing stores and men of the reinforcement forces, was the target of Henderson Field bombers and took a bomb which resulted in her scuttling. *Aoba*, despite the 40 hits in her, struggled into Rabaul at high speed, thence homeward for major repairs. *Kinugasa* and *Hatsuyuki*, the former unharmed and the latter sustaining only minor damage, returned almost immediately to active duty.

At Guadalcanal, Admiral Scott was the man of the hour and *Boise*, detached and sent to the Philadelphia Navy Yard, was the ship of the hour. However, for reasons of security, details of the Cape Esperance battle were withheld from the American public which, hearing only of *Boise*'s exploits, hardly realized that there were other warships fighting that night.

Nonetheless, Savo was an American victory in the sense that the opening naval round of the Guadalcanal campaign was avenged. Conversely, Cape Esperance which saw the IJN forces defeated was a corresponding victory for the enemy forces; their mission—covering landing of troops and supplies—had been accomplished. At Savo, Mikawa never attained the goal of finishing off Turner's transports.

The Navy's fortunes were on the rise. Cool, determined Rear Admiral Norman Scott had won an important victory at sea. Their fortunes would continue to rise from this point onward.

GUADALCANAL BLUES

FOR UNITED STATES forces at Guadalcanal, the 72 hours following Cape Esperance were dark and explosive.

On October 13, Admiral Turner's transports were seen approaching the roadstead with replacements for a number of Marines. These were the 164th Infantry Regiment of the American Division and while, in a few hours time, these troops would be greeted effusively by the Imperial Japanese Navy, Guadalcanal for the moment was quiet. On Henderson Field were parked about 90 operational fighters, bombers and dive bombers. Were the Japs licking their wounds at the head end of The Slot? Navy men wondered, yet felt certain that the tide had finally swung.

This, alas, was not so. The battle in the Santa Cruz Islands was still thirteen hectic days away—memorable days for the defenders of Guadalcanal. And as for the Japs licking their wounds, this too was not so. Unfortunately, other things were in the wind.

Twenty-fifth Air Flotilla at noon provided the first of these 'other things' in the form of 24 bombers which visited Henderson Field. The unexpected arrival of these planes and their equally unexpected bombing accuracy, provided some anxious moments for Seebee groundskeepers. In the evening, enemy heavy artillery opened fire from well-concealed positions beyond the Matanikau. The net effect of these enemy onslaughts were, so far as Henderson Field was concerned, totally horrendous. By the time the bombers were gone and the artillery fire was silenced, the airfield was pitted beyond recognition.

But the enemy was still warming up and even while his guns were plastering Henderson, a powerful bombardment force headed by battleships *Haruna* and *Kongo*, with cruiser *Isuzu* and six destroyers in screen, was coming down The Slot determined to put Henderson Field out of commission for all time. In charge of this impressive array of gunfire was Vice Admiral Takeo Kurita. Tough, implacable Combatdiv 3 flew his three-starred flag aboard the *Kongo*, a 27-year-old veteran which, with *Haruna*, would provide a calling card in the amount of sixteen 14-inch guns. Aboard the two battleships were 900 rounds of AP and HE explosives, and it was Kurita's intention to dish out every last round before leaving Guadalcanal.

In the foxholes and along the perimeter, the green troops of the 164th spent the early evening thinking about Jap bombers. Their first day had been marked by a second flight of planes coming in during the afternoon. What else was in store for them? they wondered uneasily. Would a night strike come down?

"It was a helluva first day!" Lieutenant Colonel Jason Wicks recalled 20 years later. "All we kept thinking about was those bombers—nobody but the Marines ever gave a thought to bombardment from the sea . . ."

As the hands of the clock moved around to October 14, Admiral Tanaka's task force approached the objective. Search planes were sent aloft and a few minutes later, Japanese pilots were droning over Henderson

Field. About this time, the artillery from the hills began and as quickly as the first shells dropped in, the pilots released their flares. Eerie blood-red lights floated down to bathe the airfield. Tanaka's gunnery officer passed the word to stand by for main battery. On the darkened bridge of the *Kongo,* the sound of ship's bells wafted out to the admiral. It was 1 A.M. and the force was in bombardment position.

"Commence firing, Commander Yanagi!" Tanaka snapped. "Make them all count."

Yanagi did his best.

For 90 minutes the armor piercing and high explosive shells rained down on American positions around the airfield, abetted by the slugging capacities of the cruiser and three destroyers. The airstrip and surrounding buildings quickly became a flame-gutted shambles, and the replacements from the 164th had their indoctrination to the hell of Guadalcanal. Letup finally came when four PTs from Talagi were ordered out to attack the bombarding force. But the PTs were hardly a match for the screening ships, and the slugfest ended in a standoff.

It did, however, make Admiral Tanaka aware of the possible danger to his force of remaining too long offshore. At 2:20 A.M., his shells almost expended and his force intact, the admiral broke off the engagement and slipped around Savo Island, his force retiring at 25 knots. It was a good night's work, and well done: 41 Americans dead, 48 planes out of the original 90 beyond repair; Henderson Field finished for the time being. In the morning, as Marines searched for their dead and Seebees desperately strove to patch the airstrip, a Marine colonel arrived from divisional headquarters and made a short announcement:

"There's enough gasoline for one mission against them. Load your planes with bombs and go out and hit them with the divebombers. After the gas is gone we'll have to let the ground troops take over. Then your officers will attach you to some infantry outfit. Good bye and good luck."

Tortured Henderson Field took another enemy bomber strike about noon and another shortly after. If there had been any remote hope of fixing up the field, there was none now. The Seebees put down a grass strip and prayed for the best.

"This was about the worst of the Guadalcanal fighting for us," a Marine fighter pilot recalled. "We really didn't think the strip could be held under such conditions." Admiral Morison refers to this phase in about the same candor: "The men knew that they could not stand many more such drubbings. For the rest of the war Guadalcanal veterans would talk of Kurita's shelling as 'The Bombardment,' as if there had never been any other."

Admiral Yamato was encouraged. The next night he successfully sent down the final contingent of Hyakutate's troops and bombarded again, but this was a light, once-over job when compared with Mikawa's cruiser bombardment planned for the following night: 752 shells from cruisers *Chokai* and *Kinugasa*. On October 17 cruisers *Maya* and *Myoko* paid a visit and dropped 1500 shells of eight-inch caliber. Somehow, Marines hung on. In Rabaul, Yamato was enunciating the seventh chapter of his Analects:

"When fighting a powerful force, one must hit when its morale ebbs . . . A force's morale is keen when it sorties, gradually begins to flag, and ebbs when it is ready to return to camp. One should avoid a force while its morale is keen, and one should hit when its morale ebbs."

Japanese forces continued their slugfests almost daily, small, costly affairs that left Admiral Nimitz wondering if Gadalcanal could indeed hold out. His commander in the South Pacific, Ghormley, meanwhile, was under constant bombardment for his failure to land sufficent troops and supplies, and for the loss of so many warships around Ironbottom Sound. Ghormley, more severely criticized than any other commander in the campaign— and lastingly so by history—received this criticism in the form of a replacement. On October 18, after a conference with his staff, Nimitz reluctantly named a new commander of the South Pacific—Vice Admiral William F. Halsey, a man chosen primarily for his aggressive leadership and for the confidence he could instill in embattled American forces.

(Writing his history of the Navy in World War II many years later and before the truth was clearly known, Captain Walter Karig charitably attributed Ghormley's recall as a *serious illness*. The illness was Guadalcanalitis, and everybody, of course, had it bad. But Ghormley was top commander and therefore the chief scapegoat.)

Nimitz, in addition to this change in leadership which Halsey remarked had left him with a feeling of "astonishment, apprehension and regret," made other changes and moves. Vice Admiral Fletcher was shifted from the area and in his place was Rear Admiral Thomas C. Kinkaid, a battleship man now "getting the feel of a flattop under his feet." Battleship *Indiana* was sent through the Panama Canal with orders to stop off at Oahu and pick up the 25th Infantry Division; 50 fighter planes were ordered down from the Central Pacific; 24 Flying Fortresses and 24 submarines were ordered into the area and, in general, the wheels began to turn.

Hyakutate, meanwhile, had gotten an estimated 22,000 troops moved to Guadalcanal and was girding his loins. So was the Imperial Japanese Navy. Another Naval battle for Guadalcanal was in the wind and Yamamoto's commanders, plagued by a great number of deficiencies of their own, paradoxically dreaded a showdown almost as much as they'd looked forward to cleaning the South Pacific of the United States Navy.

In Noumea, the new commander of the naval forces called a conference. Vandergrift flew in to attend. Asked Halsey:

"Are you going to evacuate?"

"Negative," replied the Marine general. "I can hold but I've got to have more active support than I've been getting."

"All right," Halsey said. "Go on back. I'll promise you everything I've got."

He then backed up his word by sending Rear Admiral Willis A. Lee and his *Washington* force to prowl east of Savo Island.

On Guadalcanal, the night of October 24-25, the Japanese Army launched its all-out offensive against the Marines. Chesty Puller's people and the raw 164th dogfaces made the night an epic one in a desperate bid to keep the enemy from overrunning American positions. It was the night for which Sergeant John Basilone received the Congressional Medal of Honor, Puller the first of his four Navy Crosses. The enemy attempted four separate attacks and was repulsed at great cost, but Marine and Army casualties were also heavy. The Navy, at this time, was fighting minor skirmishes of costly nature off Talagi. However, the indecisive state of affairs for both the Japanese and the Marines on Guadalcanal, was about to come to a screeching halt as Admiral Yamamoto's patience was at an end.

The commander in chief of the IJN "warned the army that the fleet was running out of fuel and would have to retire unless Henderson Field were captured." It was not, and the Japanese admiral made his move. But a premature report from the admiral's naval liaison officer on Guadalcanal at 1 A.M. October 25 started the wheels in motion for the Japanese Navy's southwestward rush.

Admiral Yamamoto (commanding a force of 4 carriers, 5 battleships, 14 cruisers and 44 destroyers) directed carrier *Junyo* to make air war on shipping at Lunga.

While Japanese commanders were concerned about the location of American carriers, and were still trying to puzzle the mystery of the grandoise claim from Guadalcanal, IJN warships were on the move. Admiral Nagumo's powerful carrier force had a bad scare when a fighter circled the force and signalled that it had shot down an American plane. In fact, Nagumo had almost made up his mind to double back when further scouting reports cancelled his intentions. There were no American carriers in striking range. Nagumo breathed a sigh of profound relief—he'd been at Midway when there were.

At 20 knots, the IJN moved toward Guadalcanal and a tactical victory.

PART IV

Santa Cruz Islands

AT MIDNIGHT plus ten October 26, a far-ranging PBY broke radio silence with a report for Admiral Kinkaid's carrier force: enemy fleet sighted, distant 300 miles. Three hours later, another PBY announced an even more precise and startling disclosure: enemy fleet consisting of a carrier and six other vessels 200 miles from Task Force 16. In Noumea, Vice Admiral Halsey was broken out. He checked the messages received there after 5 A.M., because of a communications failure, and after stepping off distances to Kinkaid's carriers sent the following message:

"Attack—Repeat—Attack!"

Kinkaid was waiting for just such an order. With two powerful carrier groups, one built about the hastily-repaired *Enterprise* and the other around *Hornet,* the old battleship admiral was patrolling in the waters northeast of Guadalcanal waiting for something to break. And when it did, Kinkaid was ready. Directing Captain Osborne B. Hardison of *Enterprise* to send aloft Bombing Squadron 10 and Torpedo Squadron 10, to launch a 200 mile search, the carrier turned into the wind and launched 16 SBDs armed with 500 bombs "just in case."

Pairing up, the SBDs roared off on a SW by W track. First to contact the enemy were Lieutenant Vivian W. Welch and Lieutenant (jg) Bruce A. McGraw, USNR. At 6:17, after sighting an enemy "Kate," the pair sighted the advance echelon of the Japanese force. At 6:30 they radioed their findings, searching further but failing to uncover additional Japanese forces. On their return to *Enterprise,* the lieutenants sighted the same Kate apparently returning from a similar mission over Kinkaid's armada.

The Japs were coming in three groups: an advance force consisting of a carrier, two battleships, with destroyers and heavy cruisers; three carriers and their escorts; and a rear force of two more battleships, heavy cruisers and destroyers.

Lieutenants Welch and McGraw had merely sighted one-third of the total enemy potential. Another third was located by Commander James R. Lee and Lieutenant (jg) William E. Johnson—the carrier force. Here were *Zuikaku* and *Shokaku,* their decks empty, awaiting the arrival of *Zuiho.* The enemy had his combat air patrol up and the Zeros promptly waded in. Lee took one under fire, Johnson two. Then both planes lit out for home. But Lieutenant Stockton B. Strong and Ensign Charles B. Irwin, a hundred miles away, heard the contact report from these planes, and turned around to link up.

By now *Zuiho* had linked up with the main carrier group and it was she who received the brunt of the American airmen's attack when it finally came . . . "Two enemy scout planes cut through the overcast and suddenly swooped to spray a few bombs on carrier *Zuiho,*" reported Captain Tomeichi Hara, skipper of one of the flattop's escorts. "Their daring raid paid off. One bomb pierced the flight deck aft and exploded. The resulting fire was soon put under control but the deck was ruined. The carrier's skipper signaled that she could launch planes, but could not receive any on her damaged deck. Admiral Nagumo reluctantly ordered *Zuiho* to withdraw after dispatching all of her fighters."

The American version of this hit-and-run is essentially the same, except wherein the enemy admits no plane losses. There were at least two, as aviators Strong and Irwin tangled with Zeros and then, taking advantage of cloud cover, streaked away unharmed.

On the *Enterprise*, Admiral Kinkaid received word that enemy carriers had been found and ordered an attack from both his command carrier and *Hornet*. These planes—two from *Hornet*, one from Big *E*—left in three waves, each proceeding independently with the *Hornet* group in the lead. Meanwhile, the other planes of the original search, finding no targets in their assigned areas, streaked off to find and unsuccessfully bomb cruiser *Tone*.

Hornet's first group was jumped by a dozen Zeroes, which came at them out of the sun. However, after recovering from initial shock, the Americans tore into the enemy fighters and shot down 10 of them while *Enterprise* torpedo planes were virtually wiped out by the tidal wave of planes that engulfed them. The other American air groups clawed their way toward the enemy carriers, through the melee, through the flak thrown up by battleships and cruisers of the first force and eventually found targets. But, so did Japanese planes.

Shokaku, Azukaku and *Zuiho* (now out of the running) had thrown aloft a 65-plane strike; carrier *Junyo*, in the rear was readying a 29-plane strike and, even as the American torpedo planes were approaching, another 44 planes surged up from the two operational Japanese carriers.

Now both carrier commands awaited attack. The Japanese strike, launched first, arrived first. Kinkaid's *Enterprise* was ringed by *South Dakota*, cruisers *Portland* and *San Juan*, and eight destroyers. Ten miles distant was *Hornet* with attendants. A combat air patrol of 38 planes circled in layers, impatiently waiting 10 miles out for something to happen.

It did, and fast, but not to the Big *E*.

Over *Hornet* planes were suddenly dogfighting with enemy fighters as dive bombers prepared to work the flattop over with bombs. Combat air patrol attempted to intercept but most efforts were too late. The enemy had gotten off his strikes first. He had to jump. *Hornet's* planes had to scratch for altitude even as the advance echelon of the enemy strike tipped over to lay eggs. Admiral Murray, commander of this group of ships, rammed out a lively antiaircraft fire but to no avail. The bombs were raining down even as Jap aircraft slewed apart in midair, and the first bomb hit the starboard side of *Hornet's* flight deck aft. Then came a pair of near-misses parallel to the bridge, hammering the hull. Next came a dive bomber clawing through the flak, guns firing, to crash into the stack. Bouncing off, he tore through the flight deck where his bombs exploded. His original glancing blow had doused the signal bridge in gasoline and had left that area in flames.

Enemy torpedo planes skimmed in low, astern, next. All guns swiveled around, but two hits on *Hornet's* engine rooms were already registering. These hits finished all power and communications, throwing the carrier into a 10 degree starboard list. A cloud of smoke, steam and flames spiraled skyward as three more bombs were dumped accurately on crippled *Hornet*.

The first exploded on impact; the second ploughed through four decks before its fuse touched off; the third detonated in the forward messing compartment, starting fires and killing a number of men. Lastly, a torpedo bomber took dead aim on the bow of the burning carrier and crashed in flames into the port forward gun gallery and there exploded.

But there were other warships in this ball game, and these, too, came under simultaneous attack. Destroyer *Mustin* scratched a torpedo bomber with her 20 mm guns. Another, diverted from *Hornet,* singled out *Pensacola* and attacked her, only to be shot down in flames by her hot gunners. A third torpedo plane singled out twisting tinclad *Anderson* but was spilled close aboard by her persistent 20s. Most of the enemy planes singled out the carrier, of course, and at battle's end 25 out of 27 were shot down.

However, *Hornet* was dead in the water, and fighting fires which threatened her very existence.

At this moment, her air groups led by Commander Gus Widhelm were approaching the Japanese force. Her 15 dive bombers and four fighters had refused Admiral Kondo's bait, passing over the capital ships in the advance echelon of the three waves in order to attack the carriers. Kondo's combat air patrol had engaged and two Navy fighters were lost in the melee, but the others held their course and soon found paydirt. It was 9:30 A.M. when flattops *Shokaku* and *Zuiho,* the latter smoking profusely from her earlier encounter with American carrier planes, were finally sighted by *Hornet's* air groups.

Eleven planes bored through the flak and the swarm of attacking Zeroes to pushover point. The rest crashed in flames or ditched, as did Commander Widhelm. From the perspective of a life raft he watched his torpedo bombers drop four 1,000 pound eggs on the carrier's naked flight deck. Crippled and smoking, *Shokaku* like *Zuiho,* was out of the war.

"I saw two enemy bombers pierce *Shokaku's* gunfire and dive full toward the carrier from a height of about 700 meters. The planes arced up at the last moment and disappeared into the clouds. The next instant I saw two or three silver streaks, which appeared like thunderbolts, reaching toward the bulky carrier," Captain Hara recalls. "Their impact raised flashes at the fore and amidship, near the bridge, of *Shokaku*. The whole deck bulged quickly and burst. Flames shot from the cleavages. I groaned as the flames rose and black and white smoke came belching out of the deck. The flagship was hit at last—and how vulnerable it was—by four bombs!"

Zuikaku, the only operational carrier in Nagumo's force, received a signal to clear the area with all haste. She would have to carry the workload of landing three carriers' groups, and this was an impossible load to shoulder. Carrier *Junyo* was not part of this force, the flattop having originally been ordered into Kondo's advance force. Nevertheless, the two enemy carriers having learned of the presence of a second American carrier (*Enterprise*) in the area, decided now to go for broke. Other assaults were quickly launched.

At about this time, *Hornet's* second wave was coming in. But this one missed the carriers completely and had to settle for *Chikuma,* of the Kondo group. Two bombs devastated her bridge, a third pierced her decks and near-misses sprayed her superstructure. *Chikuma* was out of the fight and headed for the barn. Cruiser *Tone* fared well, however. Her capable ship handling and fine gunnery department brought her out clear of the fiery chasm, while battleship *Kirishima* also defended herself well against SBD attacks.

Meanwhile, a thousand men labored to save the burning *Hornet.* Destroyers *Morris* and *Mustin* were ordered alongside to pass hoses. The former, alongside first, passed three which were hauled across the flight deck and used to combat the fire on the port side. *Mustin,* coming up on the port quarter, was joined by destroyer *Russell* on the port bow, both passing and operating hoses in a desperate effort to save the cripple. *Hornet's* plight was not irremedial at this point. Commander Henry G. Moran, damage control officer, managed a quick control of the fires by a liberal use of chemical "foam" and CO_2 extinguishers, in addition to the tons of water coming aboard from the destroyers.

Could the engineering department do anything about getting up steam? Commander Edward P. Creehan's Black Gang was willing to try. Engineers were scurrying around blackened spaces trying to work their miracles, perhaps even seeing a way out of their predicament. Admiral Murray and his staff were taken off by *Russell* and transferred to cruiser *Pensacola,* now the flagship for the *Hornet* group.

As *Russell* moved back to the stricken carrier, cruiser *Northhampton* was ordered to take *Hornet* in tow. She'd already missed getting plastered by an egg as an enemy dive bomber attacked her during the first towing interlude. But by 11:30 she was back, ready to try again. *Russell* and *Hughes,* meanwhile, had begun to remove the badly wounded personnel of the carrier. It wasn't until 3:40 that *Hornet* began to move—crawl—at the end of *Northhampton's* line at 3 knots.

But, here, fate intervened.

Six Jap torpedo planes, coming in low, attacked the carrier. *Northhampton* dropped the tow and began to take evasive measures as torpedoes slashed in alongside. The fish directed at the cruiser missed, but the ones for *Hornet* did not. One big hit landed on her starboard side. Then, to finish off an unhappy event, six horizontal bombers came out of the overcast to drop more lethal eggs. Most of them missed, but again the job only called for one bomb, well placed. And between the six planes, they made that hit. *Hornet's* skipper, Captain Charles P. Mason, forthrightly ordered her abandoned.

Mustin was called in for the *coup de grace.* Of eight well-placed fish, only three hit, and *Hornet* refused to roll over and disappear. *Anderson* was ordered to fire her nest of torpedoes—six of them, hot, straight and true. But the carrier which had taken Doolittle on his Tokyo junket still tenaciously clung to life. Gunfire was ordered, *Mustin* and *Anderson* together poured almost 500 rounds of 5-inch into her. Still she floated, flames and explosions tearing her apart at 10:40 P.M., when the two tinclads abruptly took off. Overhead, Jap planes were circling.

Nagumo sent in a destroyer division to catch the enemy tinclads, but *Mustin* and *Anderson* got away unharmed. Then the Japanese admiral, enjoying the spectacle of a burning, abandoned American carrier, finally performed the *coup de grace* himself. Four Long Lances speared out from the tubes from *Makigumo* and the gallant flattop heaved convulsively and sagged back in her death throes.

Enterprise, too, had struggled long this day.

In the early morning, warned by *Hornet's* first flight, *Enterprise* had augmented her combat air patrol with additional F4Fs. In one of these planes was Lieutenant Stanley W. Vejtasa, a group leader, who took off and streaked toward *Hornet* to assist in forestalling the Jap attack which was now coming in.

Vejtasa and three fighters climbed to 12,000 feet, suddenly noticing Japanese dive bombers coming out of cloud cover and reaching the push over point. When the enemy started his dive, Vejtasa was waiting. The plane emerged from a cloud and the American airman closed at full throttle, guns blazing. Scratch one. But the other bombers completed their dives and were now pulling out. Vejtasa roared off in pursuit, closed the gap and again triggered a long burst. Scratch two more.

The fight reached a lull and Vejtasa and company climbed back to 10,000 feet to await developments. In *Enterprise,* a fighter-director team suddenly announced that 11 torpedo planes were heading for the carrier. "Let's go get 'em," the carrier pilot growled over the intercom. "Follow me."

The F4Fs tipped over into a screaming dive. Jap bombers were deploying for attack position. The American planes hit them on the run and two Kates, one by Vejtasa and the other by his wingman, plunged into the South Pacific. Now a bomber was making his run on *Enterprise* and the young lieutenant whipped around to intercept. In this he was successful too, for the enemy plane dropped no bombs and instead burst into flame and flew on a few moments before crashing headlong into the destroyer *Smith*.

Vejtasa watched unhappily and then climbed back into combat air patrol position. Two more bogies were coming in, the fido team snapped. Vejtasa squinted down, saw a F4F tangling with the further plane, saw that no one had yet engaged the closer aircraft. Again he obliged. Firing in short bursts because his ammunition was nearly expended, Vejtasa emptied his guns into the bomber. Day's score: two dive bombers, five torpedo bombers, one assist on a torpedo bomber. Navy Cross for Lieutenant Stanley W. Vejtasa.

But *Enterprise* herself was almost as skilled. About 10 A.M., a Japanese I-boat stuck her periscope aloft and viewed the scene with relish. It was *I-21*, a veteran of the Guadalcanal campaign, but a sub for whom paydays had been few and far between. Out spewed four torpedoes and, to the skipper's amazement, the bulky flattop adroitly combed the wakes. He swung for a stern shot but there wasn't time. As he went deep, rigged for depth charges, his tin fish missed the carrier and ploughed into the firerooms of the destroyer *Porter*. Escorts swarmed over the spot from where the feather wakes originated, and a wise submariner headed for the bottom.

Death was an ironic twist for tinclad *Porter*. Flagship

108

of Captain C. P. Cecil, Comdesron 5, the can had been standing by with itchy guns when *Enterprise* ordered her to heave to and cast around for a downed pilot and a gunner off the flattop. *Porter* complied, and it was during the execution of this mercy mission that death waved its rattle. The torpedo hit amidships, in the fire-rooms, and killed 11 men outright. Steam and oil spewed from her sundered plates.

Destroyer *Shaw* moved to *Porter*'s assistance, and while the doomed vessel's gun crews were hammering away at Jap torpedo bombers, her damage control crew worked feverishly to square her away below. But the can was sinking and it quickly became evident that only re-moval of her ship's company remained for *Shaw*. This was accomplished in jig time and then *Shaw*, finding that her wounded companion was another *Hornet* refus-ing to give up the ghost, poured 5-inch explosive into her until she finally departed.

Now deprived of the firepower of two of her escorts, *Enterprise* prepared to go it alone as 24 enemy planes struck in a well-coordinated attack. Sporting an assem-bly of the new 44 mm mounts, Admiral Kinkaid's flag-ship made an epic fight of it with battleship *South Dakota* and cruiser *San Juan* at her side. "A solid sheet of flame from stem to stern," the carrier's anti-aircraft batteries scratched 7 planes in the immediate vicinity; *South Dakota* received credit for 26. The enemy, how-ever, managed to drop a few well-placed eggs and three of them smashed into the carrier.

One pierced the flight deck close to the bow almost on a center line and exploded about 10 feet abaft the for-ward elevator. Another, landing on the flight deck, broke in two and killed many men, most of them on the third deck. The third bomb was a near miss, but it frac-tured *Enterprise*'s skin on the starboard side aft, and opened seams there. Aboard the carrier were 44 dead,

75 wounded, and her survivors were desperately battling numerous fires and attempting to patch her wounds.

Then came Vejtasa's act in the skies but the one-man air arm couldn't get to all the enemy torpedo bombers. Nine of them slewed in low and dropped torpedoes on the port and starboard hand. But Captain Hardison was ready. Pushing the big carrier through torpedo wakes, he maneuvered her as nimbly as an elephant doing a ballet dance, and with notable success. Three of the fish were dubs and there hangs the tale of *Portland*'s survival of this battle. Plinked by three dummies under her armor belt, she remained in action throughout—slightly bumped but none the worse for the experience.

Destroyer *Smith*, hit in the bow by a suicide torpedo plane at this time, sidled close aboard battleship *South Dakota* to take a quantity of lifesaving foam. Yet even as the battleship's lines were quenching her fires, *Smith*'s crew was shooting down enemy planes. She was ablaze from bow to No. 1 gun, but aft her guns were blazing. This was the sort of heroism that won medals, and there were plenty passed around on the tinclad for her part in staving off eternity.

Then came the lull before the storm, a brief respite during which United States forces were repairing the damage, clearing flight decks, fighting fires above and below. When the bullhorns sounded again, Kinkaid's outfit had gotten a second wind.

They needed one.

The second section of the 29-plane *Junyo* strike abruptly tumbled out of a low overcast. *South Dakota*, in action for the first time, acquitted herself well. In addition to her earlier score, another half-dozen torpedo bombers were scratched by her hot gunnery. In the fracas, however, one torpedo bomber unloaded his eggs forward and *South Dakota* became a mass of flames around her No. 1 turret. Captain Thomas Gatch, skipper of the titan, reeled with a slab of shrapnel in his neck and had to relinquish control of Batt 2, where the executive officer stood by ready to assist. Fifty wounded, 1 dead, where the bomb hit. *San Juan* took an egg, an armor piercing job that rammed down through her decks and exploded on the ship's bottom. Control was momentarily lost but after a few anxious moments, all was clear again.

Enterprise, her fires quenched, turned into the wind to launch a fresh section of combat air patrol, at the same time taking aboard the gasless, ammo-less planes she'd thrown up earlier in her epic defense.

The shooting was over.

The opposing forces retired, the enemy turning triumphantly toward Truk after sending *Hornet* under the waves, while Kinkaid moved southward on his way toward Noumea. Of this fourth carrier battle in six months, the second of the Guadalcanal campaign, Admiral Nimitz summed up the general criticism of the Navy's part:

"Kinkaid, whose experience prior to Operation Watchtower had been with battleships and cruisers, adopted Fletcher's plan of controlling all fighter-direction from the *Enterprise,* but with less precision and certainly less luck."

PART V

Guadalcanal

IN THE United States, October marked a low point for the American people. Communique 112 from the Navy Department, announcing the loss of four heavy cruisers off Savo Island on August 9, hit the public squarely between the eyes. In Noumea, morale was at a low ebb too —but for a far different reason. Not so much a matter of American losses, it was because Vice Admiral Halsey felt thoroughly frustrated in his attempts to force a decisive action and to end for all time the Japanese threat to Guadalcanal.

Halsey had not been able to accomplish miracles in the two short weeks since relieving Ghormley. The Tokyo Express was still coming down on a greasy track each night; transports were still in jeopardy off Lunga Point, and stuffs of war were still in short supply for the fighting man. But if the vice admiral's spirits were flagging, so too were the spirits of Admiral Yamamoto.

Under tremendous pressure to bring down another division by express, Yamamoto had reluctantly agreed. He dreaded the trips, however, since Santa Cruz had robbed him of a number of carrier planes and pilots. Moreover, his men were dog-tired and his warships were in dire need of layup. He would test run an express on November 2 and if everything came off without a hitch, the balance of the division could expect to come down on successive nights. The outfit chosen to reinforce the decimated 2nd Division was General Kagesa's 38th Division, originally earmarked for the capture of Port Moresby.

Halsey, meanwhile, was racking his brains trying to think up new ways of bottling up the Guadalcanal access and to ferry in supplies. The enemy's Pyrrhic victory at Santa Cruz made it pretty plain that something new was in the offing, perhaps a new deluge of tinclads coming down in the express. At any rate, anything was better than nothing—why not bombardment of the enemy's positions?

On the morning of October 30 light cruiser *Atlanta* and destroyers *Benham, Fletcher, Lardner* and *Aaron Ward,* escorting howitzer-carrying transports, stopped off some eight hours to blister the Japs behind Point Cruz. Next morning, Marines jumped off and struck across the Matanikau River in what was the beginning of a long drive which was to end on November 3 behind Point Cruz.

The first few days of November were characterized by hard Navy punches at enemy land positions, and new Marine advances.

But beginning on November 2, 20 destroyers ferried down the entire 38th in four stages, and Marine advances stopped. The small sniping war centered about submarines and PTs until the morning of November 11, at which time it broke wide open for the three-day battle for Guadalcanal.

Admiral Turner, planning to bring up General Patch's 182nd Infantry Regiment (his 164th was already well-blooded) from Noumea in an effort to further bolster American land positions, knew well the Japanese intentions. Intelligence had told him of the coming of the 38th and of a massive attack which was planned for November 14. Reinforcements were urgently needed. Turner additionally knew that he could expect violent

113

land-based bomber attack as a softener that day, with support from the IJN in the shape of battleships and carriers. His plan revolved around the unloading of his transports by using Rear Admiral Callaghan (formerly Ghormley's chief of staff) and his support group (*San Francisco, Portland, Helena, Atlanta* and *Juneau*) to beat off air attacks with a combat air patrol from Henderson Field.

Admiral Halsey passed orders to Rear Admiral Kinkaid to bring up *Enterprise*, battleships, cruisers and destroyers. If Big *E*, Halsey said, couldn't get under way after making repairs after the Santa Cruz affair, the BBs and four tinclads would get under way for independent action under the command of Rear Admiral Willis Augustus Lee in *Washington*.

On the Japanese side, there were four battleships, eleven cruisers, two light carriers and three dozen destroyers available for the operation. Overall commander was Vice Admiral Nobutake Kondo, who expected severe opposition to the movement of his expresses at this time.

By November 9, there was no disputing the point that a major Japanese offensive was under way. Reconnaissance and intelligence had made it apparent to Admiral Turner that heavy enemy naval units were on their way southwestward. Turner knew well the pattern of Japanese things: movement of troops, bombardment by naval forces, air attack. His instructions to Callaghan covered everything that the enemy might do, and Callaghan was prepared to the nth degree.

According to the plan, the admiral was to precede the transport group with his own warships and arrive at the end of Sealark Channel two hours before midnight. Here, Admiral Scott's warships would link up. The two forces would then pass through the channel into Savo Sound, strike primarily any naval forces and secondarily

114

any transports. If none of the latter were present, Callaghan and Scott were to cover the American landings.

The plan went according to schedule, despite the snooping of Turner's force by a submarine which carried a small float plane. And although the submarine never approached close enough for torpedo fire, Turner was aware of the consequences of that sighting—a reception committee would greet his transports at Lunga Point. He was not disappointed. Nor was Scott, who expected trouble too.

At 9:30 A.M., four hours after their arrival off Guadalcanal's shores, Scott's cargo ships were attacked by nine Aichi type 99 bombers. *Zeilin, Betelgeuse* and *Libra* unloaded *post haste*, prompted no doubt by the additional presence of a dozen planes from the carrier *Hiyo*, then northwest of Guadalcanal.

At 11:27 A.M. a flight of 25 heavy and medium bombers came over the island but turned their attention instead to land installations. Thus passed D-Day, with gunners at their stations and all ships at General Quarters. When the hell was the Jap fleet coming? sailors wondered. The answer to this one came soon enough! So far, there was only one casualty as a result of the air attacks—a near miss had sprung plates of *Zeilin*, flooding her No. 1 hold, and at dusk with *Lardner* as escort she got under way for Espirutu Santo for repairs.

Other transports arrived the next day and likewise did Jap planes. Thirty-three bombers and fighters, strung out in a long line, approached from Florida Island. But coastwatchers had warned of this approach and transports were under way, with cruisers and destroyers milling around. Guadalcanal's CAP couldn't reckon with the low flying torpedo planes immediately, but ships put up such a withering and effective AA fire that the planes simply dumped their fish at random and pulled out. The few who survived the AA onslaught were caught by American fighters in the pullout—an action lasting 14 hectic minutes. The results of this raid were 30 dead men aboard *San Francisco;* a bomber had crashed into her after battle station; also some slight damage but no casualties when *Buchanan* was hit by friendly fire.

One Jap plane was seen streaking away, trailing smoke, and wobbling. It was the only one.

While this action was being fought, patrol planes on morning recco spotted two Jap battleships or heavies, another cruiser and six destroyers 335 miles to the northward. A second group of tinclads lay 200 miles to the northwest. In the afternoon, pilots reported still another group consisting of two carriers and two destroyers 265 miles to the westward. Admiral Turner immediately suspected 1) that there were other groups of warships under way which his recco flights hadn't turned up and 2) that the enemy or at least a part of the enemy was *en route* to Henderson Field to subject that piece of real estate to another lambasting. A bombardment, in his estimate, could only be counteracted by an alert group of warships intercepting. He planned accordingly. destroyers.

Radioing Rear Admiral Judson Callaghan to engage after ushering transports to a safe area, Turner left it strictly to white-haired, soft-spoken "Uncle Dan" to work out the details of the intercept. This officer in tactical command of United States forces afloat did precisely that. After the transports were clear, Callaghan, 52, moved into battle disposition B-1, with his cruisers and destroyers.

This force consisted of Callaghan's flagship, *San Francisco,* anti-aircraft cruiser *Atlanta,* flying the flag of Rear Admiral Norman Scott (the junior rear admiral), *Portland, Helena* and *Juneau.* Destroyers present were *Cushing, Laffey, Sterett, O'Bannon, Aaron Ward, Bar-*

ton, Monssen and *Fletcher.* B-1 disposition had been taken because it had worked well for Scott at Cape Esperance, and because the waters of Savo Sound were indeed restricted and created a problem for ships' navigators. The formation was a single snakelike affair, with radar ships not positioned to greatest advantage, and *Atlanta* slightly ahead of the flagship.

Callaghan, formerly Vice Admiral Ghormley's Chief of Staff, had been active during the planning and mounting out stages of Operation Watchtower. Now, after months of a desk job, as it were, his two-starred flag was flying from a cruiser at a moment when battle seemed imminent. Callaghan was delighted.

It was black and starless as ships' clocks heralded the approach of Friday, November 13, 1942. The task force was at General Quarters, but without a battle plan and all commanding officers without precise intelligence of what they might expect. The changing of the watch at eight bells brought a new duty section to the fore. "Sailors peered from darkened bridges, waited in crowded plotting rooms and sweated in stifling engine rooms, wondering what the score would be," Admiral Morison accurately recalled. On the bridge of the *San Francisco,* Daniel Judson Callaghan calmly strode the wings occasionally asking if the Combat Intelligence Center had learned anything of the enemy.

Precisely at 1:44 A.M., the radar operator aboard *Atlanta* suddenly tensed. Some blurred images were coming into his screen. Finally he called the OOD. "Sir," he reported, "there are contacts bearing 310 and 312, distant 27,000 and 32,000 yards."

The contacts were neither friendly ships nor land. The OOD promptly passed the word, and a few moments later came an order from Callaghan's flagship to change course to 310 degrees and steer to intercept head-on. Enemy disposition on their port bow, the 13 American cruisers and destroyers steadied up on a line with death.

Battleships *Hiei* and *Kirishima*, having linked up with additional destroyers for a massive strike aimed at Henderson Field, were crammed with incendiary projectiles, high explosive shells with thin-skins and fast-fuses designed expressly for a devastating raid on the airfield. In command of this vast array of firepower was Rear Admiral Hiroaki Abe, a former destroyerman known in the fleet for his "circumspection and caution."

To some degree, this was true. Abe, who'd opposed the idea of another bombing of Henderson on the theory that nobody—even Marines—stands still twice for the same kind of shellacking, never wanted to leave Truk in the first place. In the second, even during this sortie southward, he'd shown his prudent side by actually reversing course on one occasion and heading homeward before imperial logic asserted itself. There was perhaps only one justification for the raid to Abe's way of thinking—vengeance.

At the battle off Cape Esperance, the commander of the bombardment group had lost one of his closest friends, Goto, who believed his flagship had been struck by friendly shells. Before he expired, Goto groaned the word *Bakayaro! Bakayaro!* (Stupid Bastards!) and apparently his staff came home with the dying admiral's story. Abe, at any rate, was looking for Norman Scott, and therefore the raid on Henderson was really a secondary matter.

As his lookouts reported Savo Island looming out of the darkness, Abe upped speed to 40 knots and gave the order to prepare for gun and torpedo attack, his task force meanwhile fanning out in battle disposition. The two battleships were in the center of the formation, destroyers outboard and ahead to protect against the stingers of enemy PTs. Composition was in three distinct groups.

In the American task force, speed was upped to 20 knots and gunnery ranges plotted in. A surge of excitement coursed through the warships, now charging at the enemy pips. Callaghan, on *San Francisco*, delayed a commence firing order. Solutions changed, new correct ranges were ground in. Still no word from the flagship. Callaghan, wanting accurate SG radar, clung to the TBS radio consulting with *Helena* and *O'Bannon* (SG equipped) to feed him enemy bearings. Aboard the bridges of the American ships, the babble and drone of the intership radio spelled doom for many a bluejacket this night.

"At 1:42 a message came in from *Yudachi*: 'Enemy sighted,'" Captain Hara recalled. Admiral Abe's reaction was amazement and chagrin.

"What is the range and bearing?" Abe roared. "And where is *Yudachi*?"

Abe had hardly finished his outbrust when *Hiei's* masthead lookout frantically shouted, "Four black objects ahead . . . look like warships. Five degrees to starboard. Eight thousand meters . . . unsure yet. Visibility bad."

Abe smacked his forehead in a gesture of abject frustration, Hara noted.

Admiral Abe's opposite number in the American force was equally 'blind,' equally frustrated. In destroyer *Cushing*, Commander T. M. Stokes, Desdiv 10, noted abruptly that enemy destroyers were crossing his bow port to starboard at 3,000 yards. The tinclad's skipper heated the airwaves immediately, and swung left preparatory to launching a torpedo attack. (DDs sighted were IJN *Yudachi* and *Hurusame*.) Now cruiser *Atlanta* sheered hard left and Callaghan's voice boiled over:

"What are you doing?"

"Avoiding our own destroyers," came the cruiser's reply.

Again the TBS was a confused melee of voices, skippers wanting to know *who* these ships were and should a firing order be given? Finally Stokes came back on the air and requested permission to open fire. One precious minute had elapsed, during which time the Japanese understood the precise meaning of the ships ahead. At 1:45 word flashed back to Stokes from the *San Francisco*:

"Stand by to open fire!"

On *Yudachi*, Commander Kiyoshi Kikkawa was "flabbergasted to see an enemy destroyer suddenly emerging from the darkness, and bearing down to strike us amidships. I was not ready to fire. We turned frantically away, radioing the discovery to *Hiei*, but we could not give positions because we did not know where we were relative to our own forces . . ."

Admiral Callaghan was equally confused. Now eagle-eyed Japanese lookouts spotted high-sided *Atlanta*, and exactly at 1:50 enemy shutters clicked open and searchlight beams, swinging right and left, focused on the American van. Immediately came an order from the cruiser's gunnery officer:

"Commence Firing! Counter-illuminate!"

Range was down to 1,600 yards, solution set. "Fire!" bellowed grim-faced telephone talkers standing at gun batteries, and *Atlanta's* guns roared in throaty salutation. As 5-inch shells crashed down on enemy ships and promptly dispatched the searchlight, Japanese gunners slammed out a salvo of their own. Concentrating on *Atlanta*, Nip batteries roared out and a deluge of shells crashed down on Rear Admiral Norman Scott's "Lucky A." The ill-named cruiser reeled under the impact as explosions rocked her bridge, killing Scott outright as well as all but one member of his staff.

120

Then, from 'Frisco, came the long-delayed order:

"Odd ships commence fire to starboard, even ships to port."

At 1:45 all guns blazed out across the Sound. At the head of the column, Stokes got off three fish and was badly hit aft. But the big dish for Japanese gunners was *Atlanta,* and seeing the fires that their guns had set on the cruiser's bridge, they immediately turned loose torpedoes. Two Long Lances sundered the cruiser, lifting her bodily from the water. Then the ship, twisting like a pretzel, rocked crazily as water spouts founted down on her canted decks and dipped her to the gunnels.

In a corner of the bridge, the ship's mascot whimpered and snuggled up to the bloody corpse of a bluejacket. The terrier's name, ironically enough, was Lucky.

Atlanta's speed slid down to zero. Great tongues of flame enveloped her bridge and the first of an endless series of explosions rocked her already tortured hull. It was the beginning of the end, not only for *Atlanta* but for many in her company. Like frantic baitfish in a trap, the ships—enemy and foe alike—mingled inextricably. There was searchlight glare, gunflashes, explosions, torpedo spouts and—utter confusion—to mark well this night as an unforgettable chapter in Guadalcanal's bloody history.

Cushing, hit in the stern as she fired six fish by manual control, skidded right and out of formation. The fish, aimed at battleship *Hiei,* hit nothing. The blazing lights on her stern made the tinclad a focus point for apparently all Japanese gunnery. Within a few moments the gallant tinclad was a floating coffin, wrecked beyond repair.

Laffey's skipper fared little better. Swinging right to launch a pair of torpedoes, he narrowly averted a collision with battleship *Hiei,* the result of which was a liberal dose of lead from the wagon. Two Japanese main

121

battery salvos centered on this "termite," flaming her hull and making it necessary for men to prepare for abandonment. Her fish, incidentally, had been fired at too close range to arm effectively. But even as *Laffey* prepared for her doom, her machinegunners gave the wagon hell. It was a glorious moment, but a short one. Destroyer sailors swarmed over the side into the water, and when her hull exploded a few minutes later many of them were killed by concussion.

So it went, one horror after the next. On shore, Marines reported later that "all we could see was one big bitch of a fight."

On board the destroyer *Barton*, at the rear of the American column, a battered crew could testify it was every bit of that and more. The tinclad's combat time was a scant seven minutes, during which her skipper somehow managed to avoid a collision and simultaneously get off three torpedoes and a few rounds at a light cruiser (last seen in flames). But as she did, the DD swerved to avoid a Jap Long Lance and as a consequence stepped dead-on into a pair. One smashed into her forward fireroom and another into her forward engineroom. Almost immediately the tinclad broke in half and sank, carrying with her most of the crew.

Sterett and *O'Bannon*, outclassed by battleship *Hiei* when they took that titan on at 4,000 yards, knew the sensation of grabbing a tiger by the tail. Admiral Abe had difficulty locating targets at first, but three minutes of hot gunnery gave his crews a brightly burning target. That was enough for them. Major caliber fire came hurtling down through the night. The target was *Sterett*, Commander Jesse G. Coward on the bridge. The tinclad skipper, who was to survive and become one of Leyte's destroyer heroes, rapped out four torpedoes at 2,000 yards. This, despite the fact that at the time *Sterett* was ablaze in the stern and her steering gear was disabled.

O'Bannon's guns, alongside, came to *Sterett's* rescue.

But at this moment the voice of Dan Callaghan emerged from TBS sets on bridges that still floated:

"Cease firing own ships!"

The puzzling order had the effect of a blockbuster in an ammunition dump. Talkers couldn't believe their ears. Cease firing? the question shot back to the bridges. Affirmative! came the dismal reply.

O'Bannon was in the process of launching two fish at *Hiei* and the order didn't stop her. The range was 1,200 yards or less, and probably the torpedoes never armed. At any rate, the fish didn't explode on contact and both of them bounced off *Hiei*. The battleship's intercommunication setup went dead at this time, and as too many of *O'Bannon's* hits were falling, the BB retired. Her gunners, meanwhile, were desperately trying to bring up elevation but were unsuccessful; their 14-inch shells whistled harmlessly over the low-silhouetted American destroyer.

Now, *O'Bannon* swerved to avoid torpedo wakes and almost collided with the sinking *Laffey's* bow. It was at this moment that the ill-fated destroyer blew up, but most of the men in the water were far beyond the help of lifejackets thrown them from *O'Bannon*.

Admiral Abe, disgusted at the way things were going and unhappy because his flagship *Hiei* was the center of attraction for enemy gunnery, looked over the water at battleship *Kirishima*. The contrast was amazing. Sister ship *Kirishima*, 800 yards distant, was virtually unhit and even more important, her 14-inch guns were booming out in repeated salvos. Abe would have liked nothing better than to watch the battleship slug away with impunity, but his composition was badly disorganized and he felt that all vessels should retire immediately. This order shocked and amazed Japanese gunners much the same as Callaghan's did to his own task force.

San Francisco had entered the fray by taking on a "small cruiser or large destroyer farther ahead on the starboard bow," shifting fire to this ship which "was hit with two full main battery salvos and set afire throughout her length." It was at this time that *Atlanta*, dead in the sea, noted a strange ship coming up on her port quarter. The stranger, probably *San Francisco,* instantly opened fire at 3,500 yards. *Atlanta*'s hull was holed several times as 19 8-inch hits registered in quick succession, but she remained afloat as *'Frisco* abruptly broke off the engagement.

The astute Admiral Morison asks the question, "How else can one explain Admiral Callaghan's order to cease fire?"

It was during this brief lull in the battle royal that *Kirishima,* an apparently unharmed wagon, cut loose on the American flagship; and an enemy tinclad knifed across *'Frisco*'s bow to rake her superstructure with murderous fire. Cruiser *Portland,* meanwhile, had resumed main battery and was concentrating on the flaming *Hiei,* distant two miles. Fourteen of her shells ripped into the enemy battleship. Abe's gunners, recoiling from this ferocious assault, lobbed out a few salvos of their own at a closer target. On the third enemy salvo, *'Frisco*'s bridge was smashed. Rear Admiral Callaghan, the cruiser's skipper, Captain Cassin Young, and almost the entire bridge crew were killed.

Portland was still dishing it out, and American bluejackets were elated as they watched their shells bite into a flaming target. There were no thoughts of enemy torpedoes on the cruiser's bridge. Then, all at once, there was grave concern for the life of their ship as a single Long Lance ploughed through her stern. The result of the hit was a pretzeling of the cruiser. She turned in a complete circle and when finally she came out of the pirouette, there was blazing *Hiei,* distant 4,000 yards.

124

Angry gunners let the battleship have two full salvos from the forward guns before main battery stopped.

Aaron Ward's fortunes were scarcely better. Astern of *Juneau* leading the reach destroyers, her skipper, Commander O. F. Gregor found himself in the middle of the death trap and quickly resolved to extricate his ship. Somehow sheering clear, Gregor moved up at top speed to the head end of the broken formation, and there he found his battle. Gregor also found himself in a situation approximating baseball's who's-on-first play.

He was firing on a target 7,000 yards on his starboard bow when cruiser *Helena* charged across his sights. Gregor ordered cease fire and went full astern to miss colliding with the cruiser. The narrow squeak averted, the destroyerman's fire controlmen searched around for a target. The spectacle of a burning warship came into their sights. Gunners zeroed in. It was confusing business, for as the can's guns began again to thunder, this ship flashed recognition lights. Somewhat startled, Gregor looked twice. Jap warship. He belayed a Cease Firing order as the enemy ship, winking furiously at the masthead, suddenly erupted great trails of flame into the night sky and, in a roaring-steaming explosion, disappeared. Or so it seemed.

Enemy searchlights were winking out across the waters of Ironbottom Sound, so Gregor directed his main battery to put them out. Plunging ahead with guns blazing, the tinclad headed into the vortex of the battle. She'd almost caught up with the enemy targets when her dice got cold. The first shell came in and caught her director, demolishing it. Next, a cluster of heavy caliber projectiles thundered in to smash her rangefinder, cut down her radar masts, riddle her searchlights, wreck her radar room and knock out intership communications system. Nine solid hits including one beneath the waterline registered before *Aaron Ward* stopped. Even

125

with a wrecked engineroom incapable of keeping her underway, she managed, after furious attempts by her Black Gang, to crawl a short distance and out of harm's way. There she stopped again, while the crew battled flames and damage control strove to keep her alive. They succeeded.

Of all the destroyers in the American formation, only *Fletcher* came away from the battle without as much as a furrow in her hull. Equipped with the latest SG radar, this last vessel in Callaghan's force accurately pinpointed enemy targets and went to work with a vengeance. Range was 5,500 yards to the ship in her sights—the Jap who nailed *Atlanta. Fletcher*'s skipper, Commander W. M. Cole, selected this vessel for a 10-torpedo attack at 35 knots while his radar-prompted sailors flailed away on all guns. Fish away, *Fletcher* sheared clear for a breather and saw the sky suddenly glow from what was obviously a torpedo hit.

Monssen, on the other hand, drew a blank. She was astern of *Barton* when the battle opened, and when that tinclad was hit by a torpedo, she ploughed through a group of unseen survivors. At 4,000 yards, her lookouts spotted *Hiei* in the glare and flash of battle. Relying strictly on telephone and visual sightings since his radar had been damaged during an air raid the previous day, her skipper, Commander C. E. McCombs readied five torpedoes. The can bored in, firing the spread. As an afterthought, perhaps thinking of the battleship's armor belt, he drove home another spread of torpedoes. So far, so good. *Monssen* turned away. But at this moment, death intervened.

Starshells suddenly lit the air space above her, bathing the tinclad in ghostly brilliance. McCombs, erroneously thinking the shells were the product of some friendly vessel's guns, flashed her recognition lights. That was all the enemy needed. The first of 37 major caliber shells whistled down on her in an orgy of flaming steel; a spread of Jap fish was launched at the can. Sidestepping the latter, the deluge of shells ripped into the destroyer, and that was it—*Monssen* was finished.

Her 20 mm's and 5-inch batteries were still flashing as twin tentacles of light fixed her for Jap gunners. Shells ploughed into the bridge, turning it into a fiery shambles. Decks heaved up convulsively and stayed that way. Projectiles ripped into the ship's power system and smashed her pumps. Gunnery mounts, directors, ashcan racks were blown overboard, and with them the tinclad's crew. Fire and wreckage strewed the belowdecks areas as the onslaught tallied 130 dead. She was a fiery derelict. Those who were able, abandoned, but survivors in the water heard cries for help somehow coming from within her. Three sailors, Boatswain's Mate 2/c C. C. Storey, Gunner's Mate 2/c L. F. Sturgeon and Fireman 1/c J. G. Hughes, climbed off the security of their raft to swim back. Boarding the burning vessel, they braved flames, explosions and smoke to go below and rescue eight trapped men from *Monssen*'s lower compartments. Then, a few seconds after the rescue party dove overboard, the destroyer blew up and sank.

Time: 12:22 A.M., just 24 minutes after the open gun, and the Japs were in headlong flight. The sea was dotted with the fires of burning hulks, oil, human flotsam.

But the fighting was *not* over.

Aboard the Japanese destroyer *Amatsukaze*, severely mauled by American shells and with dead men littering her bridge, Captain Hara had just gotten a report from damage control: "All fires were under control. A few minutes later I saw *Hiei* to port. Her fires appeared to have subsided but the flagship was almost at a standstill. There were no Japanese ships around to offer help. I felt sorry for my friends in the doomed ship, but my ship was in no shape to help anyone. The most I could do was to keep her going in a northerly direction . . ."

American destroyer *Cushing* was one of the last to go down as a result of the main action. Most of her fires were under control and apparently she was holding her own when salvos from the battlewagons swarmed down in vengeful afterthought. Flames engulfed her. Attempts to save the destroyer were futile and she was abandoned. Fifty-nine dead stayed with the crematorium when, much later in the morning, she blew up and sank.

Cruisers *San Francisco* and *Atlanta* were in approximately the same threatened predicament. The former had been hit by 14 major caliber shells, most of them from *Hiei*. Command had devolved on the unfortunate flagship to Lieutenant Commander Bruce McCandless, himself wounded by refusing to quit the struggle. A tough little career offcer, McCandless was made of stern stuff and, despite the fires raging throughout the ship, loss of steering, topsides wrecked, he fought *San Francisco* to the end and aggressively searched out targets for her bloody gunners. Later awarded the Congressional Medal of Honor by a grateful Navy, McCandless indomitably led the struggle for the cruiser's survival.

There were other heroes this terrible night, and Navy Cross winner Captain Howard W. Westin (present rank) was among them . . . "When this battle was almost over, I spotted what looked like a heavy cruiser on opposite course, about 3,000 yards on the port beam. Just after reporting this to control forward, I saw this ship fire a salvo at us.

"As three or four shells came toward us, I could see their tracers and they were not moving to the right or left but arching directly toward us. I yelled to the lookout who was with me and told him to 'duck, here comes one!' I squatted behind a column and was facing aft when the salvo hit. An 8-inch shell landed 10 feet forward of us and exploded in the compartment below, killing about eight men.

"I was hit with shrapnel in my left hand and left knee and my leg buckled out from under me, but I retained consciousness. I soon found my telephone line was out. (I didn't see my lookout after that until 10 days later in the hospital. By this time he was walking around and he told me he'd jumped behind me facing my back. The back of his life jacket had been riddled and caught fire and a large chunk of shrapnel had gone through the cheek of his fanny.) I climbed down a 10 foot ladder by jumping from one step to the next using only my right foot and right hand. I then lay down on the deck and yelled for help . . ."

McCandless, with the able assistance of Lieutenant Commander H. E. Schonland, acting first lieutenant, conned the blazing ship along the coast of Guadalcanal. Her decks were littered with dead and dying and 23 separate fires were burning as the pair removed *'Frisco* from further harm.

Atlanta, out of running, her topsides blazing and all propulsion lost, was in worse shape than the flagship. *Helena, Juneau* and *Portland,* the latter steaming in circles with badly damaged stern, still had firepower. *Helena* and *Juneau* smashed at the enemy residue until *Juneau* took a torpedo in her forward fireroom. The effects of this fish were sufficient to convince Captain Du-Bose, her skipper, to clear the area. As he did, a few parthian salvos left his guns with excellent results. Other American ships limped toward Indispensable Strait, tossing final punches at benumbed Admiral Abe.

This gentleman, who was soon to come in for sharp criticism from fleet boss Yamamoto and, in fact, be court-martialled out of service, gathered his embattled forces together for a run-back. *Hiei,* hit by more than 50 major caliber shells, was a fiery wreck, about which were grouped three destroyers attempting to screen her from further harm. Not one of Abe's other ships had escaped damage. Two of his cans and a cruiser had been sunk, and the remainder of his recently-impressive force had been smashed up. Now these survivors limped home in bewildered retreat.

The orgy of shot and shell was over, and in battered American ranks there were concerted efforts to pick up the pieces.

As the night sky lightened and the first rays of the sun climbed Cape Esperance, a small fleet of Navy tugs came out and nestled close to the wounded *Aaron Ward*, taking that vessel in tow and returning with her to Tulagi. Tug *Bobolink* put a tow line aboard the crippled *Atlanta* and, after most of her crew had been removed, nosed her to the beach at Kukum. The morning brought air raids and the tug's crew, shooting off their guns, downed a bomber. Captain Samuel B. Jenkins, the cruiser's skipper, tried desperately to save his battered ship but the flooding within her was too great. Much later in the day sailors fashioned a demo charge and with great reluctance scuttled here.

In the battered Callaghan force, Captain Gilbert C. Hoover of the *Helena* became OTC. Leading *Juneau*, *San Francisco*, *Fletcher*, *O'Bannon* asd *Sterett* down Indispensable Strait, the ships steamed into a death trap. About 10 o'clock *Sterett* delivered a hot depth charge attack on an unseen I-boat, and, hoping for the best, Hoover's column stumbled on. The column's destination was Espiritu Santo, where Admiral Halsey's ship dispensaries offered new steel for old. It was about an hour after the first submarine alert.

Enemy I-26 poked her battle periscope up through the glassy sea—a dream setup! Cruisers and destroyers limping southward after battle! Forward torpedo doors thumped open, range, angle, depth hastily computed. Then—*fire!* Two torpedoes slashed down the track past *San Francisco*. The cruiser's lookouts saw the bubbly wake, but for lack of intership communications no tocsin alerted *Juneau,* on her beam. The fish ran straight, hot and true. One minute after the Japanese skipper had fired, a Long Lance sundered *Juneau*'s port side under the bridge. A livid tongue of flame shot skyward as a tremendous explosion and a cloud of immuring smoke covered *Juneau*'s disintegration.

"It struck amidships," recalled Gunner Alan Heyn, "because the whole thing just blew up and it threw me against a gun mount and I had one of those steel helmets on and when I came to, everything was all torn apart there, and there was oil coming down the air and I thought it was rain, but it was just oil from the boilers or something. The tanks had blew up in the air.

"And there was smoke and there was fellows lying all around there and parts of their shields torn apart and the fantail, where I was, was sticking almost straight up in the air. It was so slippery that you couldn't walk up it and the guys that was still able to climb over the side, couldn't walk up, they were crawling over the side and holding the life line trying to pull themselves further aft and jump over. And they were jumping over and bumping into each other . . ."

Captain Hoover of the *Helena,* without leaving boats or dropping rafts, sailed on. Overhead, an Army B-29, attracted by the explosion, was asked by signal flag to relay a message to Admiral Halsey's headquarters that *Juneau* was gone. Halsey, according to Morison, relieved Hoover of his command for holding course. Later Halsey, the historian records, admitted that Hoover believed he was acting properly since he had an inadequate screen and moreover believed that the B-29 would relay the message. This, of course, never happened. All but 10 of

Juneau's complement of 700 officers and men, including the five Sullivan brothers, died in the tragedy.

The decisive battle for Guadalcanal wasn't yet over.

Vice Admiral Kondo was determined to land troops and supplies on the island, despite Hiroaki Abe's failure to bombard Henderson Field. At 6:30 in the morning, Kondo's cruisers and destroyers received an urgent dispatch from the crippled battleship to come down and assist her. Kondo was disgusted but came, nevertheless. Behind him was Rear Admiral Tanka, Japan's great express engineer, and a convoy of 10 destroyers and 10 transports. In addition to his own group, Kondo prepared to absorb into his ranks the undamaged section —*Kirishima, Nagara,* and four cans—of Abe's would-be bombardment group.

In Truk, Admiral Yamamoto was furious. "The ship must be brought back at all cost!" he cried. But not even the great fleet boss could deter General Geiger's Marine pilots this morning from their appointed task. Shortly after, carrying fish and bombs, the Marines took off. About an hour later the planes tangled with a flight of Jap land-based fighters. Finally they spotted the crippled battleship. The Navy, too, got to eat dessert with a flight of 15 Avengers and Wildcats. A Marine pilot knocked out *Hiei*'s blistering AA batteries, while Navy teamed up to put two fish into her—two fish as virulent as Patterson's jabs at Liston.

Hiei, living up to the expectations of the English naval architect who designed her, refused to succumb of her wounds.

Those batteries surviving the night battle were still spitting shellfire, and she was steaming in circles because of a damaged rudder, but there was still plenty of ginger aboard. Navy and Marine Corps pilots, replenishing arms and ammo at Henderson Field, were joined in a mid-afternoon raid by B-29s from Espiritu Santo. Aviators then had a field day, pouring into the battleship a total (Japanese figures minimize the pasting) of twenty-three torpedoes, four 1,000 pound bombs and six 500 pound bombs. As three Papanese destroyers closed, the crew set off scuttling charges and *Hiei* sank stern first, five miles NNW of Savo Island.

In Noumea, Admiral Halsey was issuing orders. To Kinkaid with *Enterprise,* his word was cover the retreat of the cruisers and destroyers limping home from the night's melee. To Willis A. Lee, later in the day, orders went out to bring up battleships South Dakota and *Washington.* About 3 o'clock, Kinkaid was closing Guadalcanal at 23 knots, while Lee's group was doing approximately the same in an effort to prevent another incendiary bombardment of Guadalcanal.

But Lee's group could not be expected before 8 o'clock that night, perhaps later. And so it was—much later. The Japs were coming down with everything they had. This included battleship fire and Gunichi Mikawa, hero of Savo, who was leading a fairly potent group of cruisers and destroyers down from the Shortlands. At midnight Mikawa arrived off Cape Esperance and promptly detached the bombardment group under Shoji Nishimura while he patrolled off the island to take on any U.S. ships which might attempt interference. Then, from heavies *Maya* and *Suzuya,* belched forth 500-rounds of 8-inch incendiary projectiles.

"Of all shellings the Marines on the island had to bear this was the hardest," Pratt concludes. "They cowered in foxholes and shed actual tears, tired out."

It was 2:20 A.M. when Nishimura quit lobbing them out. He had expended his ammunition and wrecked Henderson Field, most aircraft included. Six PT's from Tulagi interfered but because of their limited capability, only one cruiser was hit. Had Callaghan's sacrifice been in vain? Our forces began to wonder.

Henderson Field had been plastered, and Tanaka was bringing up transports loaded with troops and supplies. At this juncture, everyone seriously began to doubt if Guadalcanal could really be held. However, the gloom of the night was considerably lifted the morning of November 14. From *Enterprise* had come plenty of Kinkaid's reinforcements, Navy pilots—casting their lot with Army—and Marine Corps flyboys, prepared for one of the busiest days in the chaotic history of the airfield.

Savo had taught a lesson, and well. At daybreak, as Mikawa and Nishimura were retiring up The Slot, Navy fighters and torpedo-bombers took off from Henderson Field. *Enterprise* sent aloft torpedo planes. Although Admiral Mikawa had gotten off (less *Kako*) scott free after smashing Allied heavies in Ironbottom Sound, this trip wasn't going to pan out the same way. Daylight found American planes roaring up the Sound looking for the enemy force. With antiaircraft fire blistering the heavens, *Enterprise* flyboys made the first contact.

Diving through the flak, they ripped into heavy cruiser *Kinugasa* and light cruiser *Isuzu*. Both ships were badly holed and blazing fiercely by the time Navy pilots commenced their commutation trips for more gas and ammunition. Later in the morning, an *Enterprise* search again located the Mikawa group and added to Japanese frenzy. *Kinugasa* was left down by the head and listing sharply. There was still more to come.

Navy, Army and Marine Corps squadrons found a veritable treasure trove 60 miles north of Guadalcanal. Here, like fish in a rain barrel, waited Tanka's transports. As the first of 11 Japanese marus felt the wrath of American bombs and torpedoes, badly damaged *Kinugasa* was beginning to dip beneath the South Pacific. Mikawa's retirement—unlike that first trip in August—was under intense fire all the way. Meanwhile, carrier planes battered and sank seven loaded transports in a daylong aerial blitz which ended in parthian shots by the Army and Marine Corps. It was a great day for the men of Henderson Field.

Tanaka was faced with two alternatives: he could withdraw completely, or he could take survivors aboard and plunge onward toward the bloody island. He chose the latter.

November 14 was memorable too for the surface ships commanded by Admiral Lee. He had been unable to stop the bombardment of Henderson Field for the simple reason that at the time, *South Dakota* and *Washington*, with destroyers *Preston, Walke, Gwin* and *Benham* were better than 300 miles from the scene. At dusk of the 14th, Lee was off Guadalcanal praying for the arrival of the Japanese force which was reported 150 miles to the north. These were the warships of Nobutake Kondo, with remnants of Abe's fleet, battleship *Kirishima*, and his own heavy cruisers *Atago* and *Takao*, two light cruisers and a destroyer squadron. Kondo's mission was the obliteration of Henderson Field—the big thorn in the Imperial Japanese Navy's side.

It was clear and bright, sea calm, that November 14, when Rear Admiral Willis Augustus Lee went hunting.

His six-ship column, granted operational freedom by Admiral Halsey, was off the western end of Guadalcanal hoping to keep a date with enemy surface ships. Guns were loaded, gunners fired up to the proper key for *the* night battle of Guadalcanal.

In the chart houses of battleships *Washington* and *South Dakota,* navigators cursed the restricted waters of Ironbottom Sound ahead. It was tough enough with tin-clads, but maneuvering BBs was downright rough. Lee, 52, Annapolis '08, saw by moonlight the distant hulks

135

of burning enemy transports. He turned the column toward Savo Sound, waters through which he had passed earlier.

It was 9:48, and on radar sets, the shoreline of Guadalcanal came up as a long, irregular pip, and next the smaller island of Savo. The night was sufficiently bright to see patroling PTs from Tulagi, and two of them were far ahead of the column, moving slowly across the Sound. Lee came in from the open bridge and stood beside the TBS set. From the wing came the word that the PTs were closing fast. At the same time, radar picked up the impulse created by three enemy ships.

Lee snapped up the receiver. The PTs were talking to Tulagi, reporting his presence, and discussing amongst themselves the identity of these "big ones." Lee wanted to get the dope on the three pips from Vandergrift himself. Failing this, he issued the most dramatic order of the war:

"This is Ching Lee. Get the hell out of the way, I'm coming through!"

Splinterboat skippers breathed a sigh of relief and backed off, for battleships slightly outclassed the President's tribe. Three pips now became four (*Sendai* and three destroyers, one of Vice Admiral Kondo's triple-pronged attack that night), and Lee pushed up his speed and nudged through the hole toward Ironbottom Sound. Two minutes evanesced in dead silence aboard *Washington* as radar operators riveted their eyes to the enemy impulses.

Lee called *South Dakota* and the four destroyers, telling them to fire when ready. His own battleship was the first to comply with the order. The target was an enemy can, third ship in the column. *South Dakota*'s first 16-inch salvo fixed *Sendai*. Four minutes after the BBs cut loose, the cans chimed in.

Rear Admiral Shintaro Hashimura, commanding this

sweeping group, was thunderstruck by this reception. He expected trouble, but not so soon. As *South Dakota*'s second salvo appeared to fall on target, Hashimura ordered his stunned force to barrel out at high speed. But there were other Jap targets for Task Force 64 this night and six minutes later, at 1:22, *Walke*, ranging out from the American column saw destroyers hugging the shores of Savo Island.

These were destroyers *Ayanami* and *Uranami*. Now Rear Admiral Kimura and his group of destroyers and cruiser *Nagara*, Kondo's advance guard, joined the fray. Japanese tin fish slashed overboard and sped along their deadly track. Next the enemy unleashed his main battery.

On the receiving end, American destroyermen were keeping busy too. Leading Lee's column, *Walke* opened first fire and a fraction of a second later *Benham*'s 5-inchers barked angrily. The first salvos were directed at the enemy ships standing out from Savo, then as the flash of guns seared the night other Jap ships were seen to the left and the American destroyers swiveled left also. Chief Fire Controlman R. P. Spearman of *Walke* said:

"The range was about 14,000 yards but the ranges came down very fast. I don't remember what it was when we ended up, because I wasn't near the rangefinder, but I know it was point-blank. The Gunnery Officer said, 'We'll take the bridge off that ship,' so we went through 250 rounds into that bridge. The *South Dakota* got three salvos out and the third hit the magazines in the stern of the Jap, and it looked to me like it went 500 feet up into the air!"

This was the moment that *Walke* was smothered by a deluge of enemy shells, and she slid off to one side of the column, still shooting off her guns. *Benham* wanted to shoot torpedoes, but refrained from doing so, although

137

her guns were beating out a hot tattoo. Destroyer *Preston*, firing at the best opportunities, was suddenly hit on the port side by three cruiser shells. These promptly put her out of action, and started huge fires on the after end of the ship. The holes in her, admitting the sea, sent her listing hard to starboard. *Preston*'s stern settled fast, and at this point Commander Max C. Storms, her skipper, ordered an abandonment. Thirty seconds later she began to sink. The very last thing that her survivors saw was the knife-edged bow rising vertically in air, slowly inching under like some weird symbol of all the dead ships in Ironbottom Sound.

Weird, too, was the exit of *Gwin* from the fighting. Fourth destroyer in the line leading Lee's battleships, *Gwin* had fired star shells to illuminate *Sendai,* then switched her fire to *Nagara.* The result was havoc for the enemy cruiser and for Lieutenant Commander J. B. Fellows' tinclad. First a shell burst in the engineering spaces, another clipped her mainmast, a third ripped into the fantail, another into the torpedo nests which dumped the torpedoes out of the tubes. *Gwin* shook herself groggily, staggering ahead, but the shellacking she'd received was too much. The destroyer dipped her beam-end under, and she was out of the battle. Heavy-caliber shells screamed overhead as Fellows conned her toward Cape Esperance and out of harm's way.

Benham, at the business end of the American column, had worse luck. Only 300 yards from *Walke,* she took her cue from that destroyer and probably had at *Nagara.* Lieutenant Commander John B. Taylor, saving his fish for the propitious moment, never realized an opportunity to shoot them off. For a few moments after the battle broke wide open, *Benham* was the unfortunate victim of a deadly Long Lance—a fish that hit her at 11:39, demolished her bow in a thundering eruption of black water and sent her reeling. When this destroyer returned to an even keel, the fight was over for her. She commenced to settle.

"It was like being on a Coney Island rollercoaster with some nut for an engineer. The ship kept twisting over one way, then another. Nobody could right her and the forward talkers were screaming that she was taking the sea," Radioman First Class J. L. Larker recalled. "I had the transmitter literally spill in my lap. It had torn free of the bulkhead and pieces of it were everywhere. Then the sea began pouring in and the old man, trying like hell to keep Damage Control on the job, finally hauled clear of the battle."

By 1 A.M., after futile attempts to succor sister ships *Walke* and *Preston*, *Benham*'s skipper needed assistance desperately. Lee provided *Gwin,* but the long trip home was too much for Navy Cross winner Taylor's tinclad and she was ultimately abandoned.

Walke's Action Report sums up the plight of the destroyermen: "The crew was organized in the water, the most seriously injured being placed on rafts. At approximately 0200 an enemy submarine surfaced close aboard the rafts and illuminated all survivors for several minutes, but proceeded without incident. An enemy destroyer later illuminated survivors . . . there was much shouting from this vessel, but she also proceeded without taking action."

The main action of the destroyers was over.

Savo Sound, filled with burning ships and oil-covered survivors drifting in small clusters, was alight with jagged flashes from the big guns of both fleets as the battle rapidly neared a climax.

From Savo Island came shells from supposed "shore batteries" and *Washington,* primarily the recipient, poured out a withering fire at a group of Japanese ships hugging the shoreline. The two American battleships were now fighting alone, without benefit of a screen. At this moment, *South Dakota*'s radar went out and radio technicians hastily went to work. She was still without "eyes" as battleship *Kirishima* and a third column of Kondo's force sailed around Savo Island.

Kondo's leading destroyers opened searchlight shutters at 5,000 yards. Salvos crashed down on the American battleship. Lee, coming to *South Dakota*'s assistance, ordered his flagship's 16-inch guns trained on *Kirishima*. Thus, while *South Dakota* was absorbing punishment, *Washington* conversely was dishing it out. As *Kirishima* reeled under the impact of American fire, she also managed to lash back with a few salvos at Lee's flagship. But the damage had already been done: nine 16-inchers, 40 5-inchers. *Kirishima,* blazing down the length of her, lost power and skidded out of the formation.

Heavy dosages of steel now poured into cruisers *Atago* and *Takao,* illuminated by their own searchlights. *South Dakota* was in a bad way too, with enemy hits aboard and her Damage Control striving to keep her tight. Her plight (radar out) was complicated further by a loss of communications and Captain Gatch, realizing what all this could possibly lead to, retired at his own discretion. *Washington* was not long in following suit. After lobbing a few salvos at a group of enemy destroyers who were hightailing it out behind protective smoke, Lee's flagship sheathed her fangs.

The battleship phase of Guadalcanal was over.

At 25 minutes past midnight, Admiral Kondo called it quits. He signalled all survivors (two of them were tailing *Washington*) and prepared to retire. In his wake was flaming *Kirishima,* exploding, tearing herself to bits. Her skipper, bearing in mind the fate of sistership *Hiei,* ordered her abandoned and scuttled as five destroyers closed to remove survivors.

At 3:25 *Kirishima* was no more.

140

Kondo's inept blocking for the IJN had resulted in disaster—four destroyers out of action, one destroyer and a battleship sunk. And yet, the final curtain had not rung down on this night. There was still Rear Admiral Raizo Tanaka, the implacable throttleman of the Express, and his destroyers and transports. Tanaka's force had been severely mauled in the daylight hours, but not sufficiently to prevent the indomitable admiral from landing troop reinforcements. At 4 A.M., as *Washington* and *South Dakota* were limping toward Noumea, Tanaka was grounding his remaining transports off Tassafaronga and Imperial soldiers were wading ashore to soon join in the land fighting for Guadalcanal.

Admiral Lee's battleship punch had scored the knockout blow, however. His column had fought with a cool, determined courage. Although none of his ships had previously operated together, they still managed to thwart IJN bombardment plans and permanently derail her long-range ambitions for this theater.

In Truk, Admiral Yamamoto took a hard look at the remnants of this fleet. Hara recalled:

"Admiral Yamamoto, who was stern with Abe, was strangely lenient with Kondo. Many of Kondo's officers were ashamed of him and themselves. They preferred not to talk about the battle."

In Washington, Admiral Ernest J. King in his report to President Roosevelt and to the Secretary of the Navy to be filed shortly, was able to say that "in spite of our losses, the battle was a decisive victory for us, and our position in the southern Solomons was not threatened again seriously by the Japanese. Except for the 'Tokyo Express,' which from time to time succeeded in landing small quantities of supplies and reinforcements, control of the sea and air in the southern Solomons passed to the United States."

141

PART VI

Tassafaronga

THERE WERE loose ends. Although the Navy had won a decisive struggle, Japanese capability remained a threat. Reinforcements were forming in the Buin-Shortlands area. On Guadalcanal, Vandergrift's bone-weary Marines were clinging tenaciously to their foothold. The long, hard road up The Slot appeared little more than a beautiful dream.

Primary objectives were obvious. Thousands of enemy troops would have to be killed or driven into the sea; the Tokyo Express would have to be derailed for all time. The attainment of these objectives was a distinct possibility now, but the planning of other campaigns was premature.

As Thanksgiving Day neared, the Marine turn-to against enemy forces got under way. Vandergrift moved his lines westward in the wake of a three-day slaughter called Santa Cruz. Here, 1,156 Japanese troops died. Marines launched a three-pronged attack, and kept on going, without artillery and naval support.

Lieutenant Colonel Evan Carlson and his 2nd Raider Battalion were present. This outfit had made the Makin Raid, courtesy of submarines *Argonaut* and *Nautilus*. The hills and ridges between the Matanikau and Kokumbona Rivers netted 400 fanatical enemy troops in a single skirmish. Complete obliteration was Vandergrift's concept, so Marines continued to fight for each kunaithatched hill, each entrenched ravine, with hand grenade and rifle—the hard way.

At Henderson Field, there were now 124 operational aircraft and these were flying daily despite shortages of gasoline. Seabees were constructing new strips and repairing old ones, and there was generally a feeling of hope for the first time. Two squadrons of PTs and a tender had come across from Panama and were patrolling nightly, ready for the Express. At Nandi in the Fijis was carrier *Saratoga*, patched up and ready to return to action; *Enterprise* was there too, all spit and polish despite a balky forward elevator. Around these flattops two new groups had been formed.

At Ulithi, home of the scarred but still floating, new task forces were getting their orders. Admiral Halsey had been promoted to four-star and had reorganized the South Pacific Area command, a vital necessity for 18 ships of the line were either badly damaged or sunk.

For about two weeks, Admiral Yamamoto kept his intentions to himself, and it began to appear to many that reinforcement of Guadalcanal was not his immediate objective. What was? On November 27, reconnaissance revealed that there was indeed more fighting in store for Guadalcanal. There were 40 barges in these upper Solomon Islands and, in addition, there were destroyers. The answer was obvious—another Tokyo Express.

It was at this time that Rear Admiral Carlson H. Wright relieved Rear Admiral Thomas C. Kinkaid, a decision of the CNP. Kinkaid had mustered a force of five cruisers and four destroyers whose purpose was to stop any new attempt to reinforce the island. Wright was a cruiser sailor fresh from duty aboard *Minneapolis*. He had but two days to become acquainted with the responsibilities of his new job, and no time whatever to plan for task force operations.

Kinkaid, on his way to command in the North Pacific,

had prepared elaborately during the lull following the Guadalcanal engagement. Lessons learned from previous battles (no more 'Roger' when 'Affirmative' is meant; searchlights only under certain conditions, and recognition signals standardized) had been incorporated into a master operations plan. But Kinkaid never got the opportunity to express himself. He was gone soon after Wright took over, and this was indeed unfortunate timing.

Two days after Task Force 67 became his command, the new custodian called for a conference of his ship captains. The yoke had been squarely thrust upon him and Wright a conscientious officer, accepted the responsibility. Present were Rear Admiral Mahlon S. Tisdale, whose flag flew from *Honolulu*, Captain Charles K. Rosendahl of *Minneapolis*, Captain William A. Kitts III of *Northampton*, Captain Robert W. Hayler of *Honolulu*, Captain Frank L. Lowe of *Pensacola* and Captain Clifford H. Roper of *New Orleans*. Also present were the destroyer skippers, Commander James E. Cooper of *Drayton*, Commander William Cole of *Fletcher*, Lieutenant Commander Gelzer L. Sims of *Maury* and Lieutenant Commander William C. Ford of *Perkins*.

This group of men met for the first time six hours before orders were received from Admiral Halsey. A concentration of six transports and eight destroyers was coming down The Slot and was expected at midnight. Task Force 67 received orders to intercept. Wright immediately put to sea.

Speed was 28 knots. Expected time of arrival was the next evening, November 30, a run of 580 miles.

Rear Admiral Raizo Tanaka, destroyerman *extraordinaire*, was the enemy's choice. Tough, durable, he had taken everything that the Navy could throw at his cans and transports in the Battle of Guadalcanal and still per-

144

sisted in the idea of reinforcing. There were few fighters of his ilk in the IJN. His men idolized him, and the United States Navy paid him lasting tribute after the war. But of his Tokyo Express, in its role as ferryboat, few of his officers had a good word.

"Ahhh," his ship captains declared according to Hara, "we are more a freighter convoy than a fighting squadron these days. The damn Yankees have dubbed us 'Tokyo Express.' We transport cargo to that cursed island, and our orders are to flee rather than fight. What a stupid thing! Our decks are stacked so high that our ammunition supply must be cut in half. Our cargo is loaded with drums which are roped together. We approach near the island, throw them overboard and run away. The idea is that the string of barrels will float and our troops on the island can tow them ashore. It is a strenuous and unsatisfying routine."

Tanaka's plan was to bring down his destroyers starting November 30, "and every four days after until December 12." The destination of the Express was Tassafaronga, near the northeast coast of Guadalcanal. Already squint-eyed, mustached Tanaka was weighing anchor from Buin for the first attempt as Rear Admiral Wright and his van were getting under way from Espiritu. The Japanese admiral's flagship was the destroyer *Naganami*, a battle-scarred veteran like himself.

At 10 o'clock that morning, Tanaka's force of ships was steaming indirectly toward Guadalcanal. Allied search planes discovered him east of Reconador Reef, stalling before he headed sharply south into The Slot. The sighting, however inconclusive, was reported to Wright, while Rabaul radioed Tanaka that there was an American task force coming up from the south. Raizo Tanaka prepared his destroyermen for the eventuality of an engagement by passing along this news.

"It is probable that we will encounter an enemy force

tonight," he said. "Although our primary mission is to land supplies, everyone is to be ready for combat. If an engagement occurs, take the initiative and destroy the enemy."

On schedule, the admiral's force of ships turned into The Slot later that afternoon. He had the dice in hand, and whether hot or cold, he intended to roll.

Task Force 67 arrived at Lengo Channel at dusk. Destroyers *Lamson* and *Lardner* came out and fell in line astern of the cruisers, somewhat bewildered by the fact that no operations plan had been communicated to them. Nevertheless, these tinclads constituted two additional obstacles to the enemy force and that was something, after all. At 10:23 P.M. the force was off Koli Point when Admiral Wright ordered a course change to 320 true. Cruisers in column, destroyers in parallel ranks, the ships steamed for another 15 minutes before a final course change.

The night was black, the sea was calm. In the radar shack on *Minneapolis*, a bluejacket was squinting into the screen trying to see ships against the sinewy outline of the big island. At 11:10, this SG-equipped cruiser found enemy pips that first came up on the screen as "a small wart on Cape Esperance." The 'wart' was 13 miles distant, breaking into individual impulses.

Five minutes later, the guns of Task Force 67 lined on Tanaka's ships, seven of them visible to radar. Voices lowered to a terse whisper and the only sound was the soft-whirring of guns in train. Throughout the warships, scuttlebutt had it that the Japs were flat-footedly walking into another trap, but this remained to be seen. Three minutes elapsed. Distance to enemy was 7,300 yards. Van destroyers readied torpedo tubes, radar-equipped *Perkins* waiting to oblige with a spread of eight deadly fish. *Fletcher* and *Drayton* were following suit.

In *Minneapolis*, Carlson Wright was listening

eagerly for the sound of float planes. His intention was to illuminate the enemy and instantly open fire. But there were no float planes overhead at this moment and ranges were coming down fast. The enemy was at 7,300 yards when Wright's voice crackled over the TBS, a question for the *Fletcher*. And then other questions and answers. The enemy was whizzing by, passing the American column on the beam, as Wright—four minutes later —told his destroyers to open fire.

Within 60 seconds of the flagship's order, torpedoes slashed out from the tinclad. Range was down to 7,000 yards as *Minneapolis* rent the night with four 5-inch salvos aimed at a destroyer. *New Orleans* followed suit. *Pensacola,* experiencing tough sledding without adequate radar, found targets by illumination with star shell, and all guns commenced action. There were eight enemy cans —*Naganami, Makinami, Oyashio, Kawagaze, Kagero, Takamani* and *Suzuke.*

Northampton and *New Orleans,* two more who experienced initial difficulty locating a target, turned combined attention to the cruiser. At this moment, *Minneapolis* zeroed in and a gas and ammo loaded Jap tinclad blew up in a sky-high show of pyrotechnics.

Wright's task force looked good. *Takamani* was bearing the brunt of American fire and there was still no reaction from Tanaka. This, it seemed, was going to be a continuation of Lee's victory two weeks earlier. Where was enemy return fire?

The answer was soon apparent in a flood of enemy torpedoes.

Tanaka's Destroyer Squadron 2, together since peacetime, had been brought up on strict Japanese doctrine. The inflexible code of the IJN held that no destroyer was to open fire with her guns in this situation but, rather, to use the gunflashes of the enemy as a point of aim in order to launch the traditional torpedo attack.

So it was this night.

With *Takamani* serving as sacrificial goat and all American guns riddling her mercilessly, Tanaka made a course change to parallel the enemy column. As he did, torpedo attack was ordered and 20 fish spewed out into the firelit waters of Tassafaronga It was Tanka's intention to hightail it away at full speed, swinging to the northwest even as his fish ripped asunder the American ships. The concept of hit-and-run was based on IJN intelligence that Tanka's force was heavily out-gunned. And bearing this in mind, the Japanese destroyerman formulated his battle plan.

Another victory at sea seemed near indeed as the Japanese bellweather absorbed a concentration of hits. Then, abruptly, at 11:28 P.M. the picture changed. Long Lance torpedoes boiled in the black waters around the bows of cruisers *Minneapolis* and *New Orleans*. Both cruisers had gotten off nine salvos, 8-inch apiece, and on the bridges there was a feeling of understandable exultation; unfortunately, this didn't last long.

Disasters struck almost simultaneously. Long Lances tore into *Minneapolis* a moment before they tore into *New Orleans*. The flagship staggered as warheads ripped into her forward compartment forward of No. 1 gun, the other into her No. 2 fireroom. A livid flame surged up on the forecastle and simultaneously a mountainou column of water rose to masthead height; amidships, fue was blazing. The water crashed down on the stricken cruiser, dousing her forward fires and subduing the other *Minneapolis* reeled drunkenly. The sea poured onto he navigation bridge—the same sea subduing the flames on deck and sending a pungent black cloud of steam toward the fantail.

Acrid fumes rolled back from the bridge—a combination of burning aviation gasoline and fuel oil. At the rupture forward of No. 1 gun, the bow section suddenl wrenched loose and dropped downward but not off. Sea spilled into the forward firerooms, drowning all hands who were trapped in the compartment. The cruiser shuddered, slowly righted herself and then, miraculously, the turrets began to speak again. Flame marked the path of shells directed by brave men unafraid in their moment of *extremis*.

Captain Rosendahl, the "helium head," who'd survive this night to become the nation's foremost exponent of lighter-than-air, found himself splashing around in a foot of water. His rifles were still slamming out shells at enemy ships, but after the 11th full salvo power failed and the turrets fell silent. The ship slowed and narrowly missed colliding with the onrushing *New Orleans*. It was then that Admiral Wright, realizing the situation was hopeless, turned over command of the column to Admiral Tisdale in Honolulu.

Next astern of the flagship was *New Orleans*, a ship without a bow. As the first torpedo smashed into *Minneapolis*, Captain Roper had ordered the wheel hard over to avoid a crash. But torpedoes were swarming all over the waters off Guadalcanal this night and, despite the turn right, *New Orleans* took a fish. The explosion caught gasoline stowage and forward magazines simultaneously, and the force ripped the bow entirely off as far back as aft of the No. 2 turret. A brilliant flash lighted the sky for a few moments and aft, a telephone talker reported that he "just saw the bow of the *Minneapolis* floating by," when he really meant the front of his own cruiser.

Power failed between bridge and enginerooms and skipper Roper, realizing that he too was out of the war, backed down from his after station to avoid other torpedoes. Somehow—mostly by guess and by God—the cruiser limped at 5-knots back into Tulagi.

Pensacola was the third ship to be torpedoed. Swung

out of line to avoid the battered twosome ahead, the cruiser was firing all guns while heading toward Savo Island. About two miles from the island another of Tanaka's stingers ploughed into steel. The fish hit port side aft and started a fuel fire—so bad a fire that hoses were burned. Immediately she developed a 13 degree list which heroic sailors corrected by pumping from the opposite side, but *Pensacola* was out of the fighting too. Veering toward Tulagi, she put into that port hours later with the fuel blaze still a bonfire.

Cruiser *Northampton* couldn't get out of her own way. Two torpedoes ploughed into her as lookouts bawled an alarm that they saw the deadly tracks. The fish took her amidships, instantly throwing up a sheet of flame and sea. When the ship stopped rolling, she began to settle into a 23-degree list from which there was no recourse. Men fought her fires bravely and without letup, but *Northampton* was doomed. At 1:30 A.M. Captain Kitts ordered everybody but a salvage crew over the side to waiting destroyers *Fletcher* and *Drayton*, but an hour later her salvage crew departed. Exactly at 3 A.M., *Northampton*, belching great billows of steam, rolled slowly over on her beam ends and disappeared.

Honolulu, Tisdale now in command, was the only American cruiser not picked off like a mechanical duck in a shooting gallery. The OTC swung around Savo Island, and spent the first half-hour firing at an old transport wreck. The enemy was hightailing it away by this time, so when Tisdale again headed north there was nothing to shoot.

But in the water there were hundreds of men and *Honolulu*, hearing their cries for help, slowed to pass through them and Tisdale ordered destroyers to the scene. *Honolulu* marched on into the early morning, hoping to catch anything enemy and catching nothing.

Only because her alert officer of the deck had swung right to avoid the three cripples ahead, instead of left, which the others had done, were the Japanese deprived of a clean sweep.

Destroyers *Fletcher* and *Drayton* made up for unhappy results with their torpedoes. Succoring some 700 men who were in the water, *Fletcher*, alone, stood by *Northampton* almost from the moment that she stopped dead in the sea and commenced her fatal list. Her whaleboat made regular commutation trips from destroyer to sinking cruiser, searching in the darkness for survivors until a load was taken aboard. Then the men from the cruiser would be taken to the destroyer, and the whaleboat would return for another load. The night abounded in courageous acts. Fireman 1/c J. E. Howell swam out to the swimmers repeatedly. Strictland, Thomas, Ryan, Krom—these were the names of others who swam through the flaming waters of Ironbottom Sound to rescue floundering cruisermen.

Drayton plucked 128 oil-covered men from the sea and brought them back for Lieutenant W. N. Pope, her Medical Officer, to patch up in a 30-hour nonstop effort.

Perkins was standing by *Pensacola*; *Maury* was with *New Orleans*. *Lamson* and *Lardner* were escorting *Minneapolis* back to the safety of Tulagi. The last named had been victims of "friendly" heavy cruiser fire which scared the daylights out of the division commander riding aboard *Lamson*, so that it took no less than recognition lights to quell the outburst.

The shooting died away. The night was over. Tassafaronga, the last major sea engagement of the Guadalcanal campaign, was history.

In Truk, Yamamoto heard Tanaka's story of a 'battleship' and two cruisers sunk, but he reserved decision pending further investigation. The Japanese propagandists claimed a great victory, neglecting to mention that no reinforcements had gotten through. America, too, claimed victory but on the basis that Task Force 67 had stopped reinforcements.

In February, Admiral Nimitz commented on the battle: "The fortunes of war and the restricted waters in which we were forced to bring the enemy into action caused our ships to suffer greater loss than their leadership and action merited, and prevented them from inflicting heavier damage on the enemy."

Raizo Tanaka, after a few less spectacular attempts to run the Express, was transferred to another theater. He had failed in his mission, Yamamoto ruled, and he was never again to hold a responsible position afloat. Captain Hara, interviewing the Japanese admiral 15 years after the war, took down these words:

"I have heard that U.S. naval experts praised my command in that action. I am not deserving of such honors.

"It was the superb proficiency and devotion of the men who served me that produced the tactical victory for us . . . but I accept the criticism of fellow officers. It was an error on my part not to deliver the supplies according to schedule."

Rear Admiral Wright accepted without reservation the full blame for the loss of one cruiser, the damaging of three others. Admiral Halsey endorsed his Action Report, faulting only the lead destroyer for discharging torpedoes at excessive range and (*Fletcher*) for sheering off to the westward without assisting the cruisers. Nobody else was blamed.

Rear Admiral Morison, official Navy historian, makes clear two points. Damage Control had greatly improved in the days and weeks following Savo. Otherwise, Tanaka's victims would likely have sunk. This was certainly true. The other:

"It is always some consolation to reflect that the enemy who defeats you is really good, and Rear Admiral Tanaka was better than that—he was superb."

The lost Japanese cause of Guadalcanal stumbled on.

PART VII

Guadalcanal Secured

ON DECEMBER 3, 1943, and for the next two months, the Tokyo Express made other speed runs on Guadalcanal but the strategic balance of the campaign was not affected.

Coastwatchers alerted Henderson Field and a reception committee of bombers was hovering over Tanaka's 10 destroyer-transports when they gave it another try. Four days later, still another reception. Net gain: 500 barrels one trip, 1500 the next. Loss to Japan: tinclads *Makanami* damaged, *Nowaki* sunk. On December 12 Tanaka tried once more. PTs were waiting and destroyer *Teruzuki* was sunk.

Moonlight and PTs kept the Express at bay until January 12. Then a nine-ship train ferried in 600 troops to cover evacuation of Guadalcanal.

Affairs on the island were now under the command of Major General A. M. Patch of the Army's XXIV Corps, and Vandergrift's 1st Division—the real veterans of the campaign—were being pulled out as fast as new troops could be brought by the Navy.

Marines had malaria, fatigue and filariasis (mumu). And guts. Together with the fresh Army outfits, they jumped off for the final drive up the coast. The army took a parallel flank. While both outfits were busy tracking and cleaning out "the ratholes" where Japs fought hopelessly until dead, Admiral Halsey, keeping the bombardment at Henderson Field fresh in his memory, handed a veritable piece of cake to Rear Admiral Waldon L. Ainsworth—bombardment of a Jap airstrip at Munda. Ainsworth, picked up by Halsey himself to lead Task Force 67 after its beating at Tassafronga, was the right man.

On January 4, Ainsworth took *Nashville, St. Louis, Helena,* and destroyers *O'Bannon* and *Fletcher* to the north of Rendova for a rendezvous with submarine *Grayback.* This was the pickleboat which had proved that major surgery could be performed under water. Three weeks before, *Grayback*'s Pharmacist's Mate 1/c H. R. Robey had removed Torpedo man 1/c W. R. Jones' appendix. Both the sub and the torpedoman were back in business at this date and looking for action. The sub was to serve as navigational beacon off the west coast of Rendova. And so she did, showing up as a pip on radar screens for surface ship navigators and then radioing that all was clear.

Navy gunners put 3,000 rounds of 6-inch and 1,000 rounds of 5-inch into an hour-long blasting. It more than evened the score for Henderson, technically speaking, but all Navy spotters could report next morning was that the field was well chewed up, although there was no evidence of antiaircraft fires. With the persistence of the enemy, this field was back in business shortly after.

At the end of January, there was another similar assignment at Vila for Task Force 67, and the results were just about the same. Submarine action at this time was moving into gear in the South Pacific. Despite torpedo troubles, American submarines were getting results.

Growler, Greenling, Guardfish, Nautilus and *Swordfish* all found good hunting in the Solomons.

Then, in February, the Japanese High Command

made its decision to evacuate. PTs and spitkits and bombers had a few days of sharp shooting, and that was all. The garrison, starving by slow degrees, was pulling out. To this end the IJN provided large groups of destroyers, as many as 18 at a clip, to take off 11,706 Army and Navy personnel.

Two-thirds of the 36,000 Japanese brought to the island remained behind, corpses all.

Three days of successful evacuation followed. Admiral Nimitz, praising the nervy operation, said "Only skill in keeping their plans disguised and bold celerity in carrying them out enabled the Japanese to withdraw the remnants of the Guadalcanal garrison."

On February 8, the 161st Infantry and 10 Marines, found empty landing boats and shattered, abandoned supplies.

Six months of terror, disease and death had cost this nation 1,592 Army and Marine dead out of 60,000 troops. Navy figures were never released. All the same, this was victory—the first leg-up on the long road back.

Paved with the bones of seamen and warships, Ironbottom Sound was now an epitaph.

Hard fighting was to continue in the Central Solomons through to the following October, but Guadalcanal—a name, an emotion, a symbol of American bravery—lay behind.

WARSHIPS SUNK

	ALLIED		JAPANESE	
	tonnage	number	tonnage	number
Battleships		0	62,000	2
Aircraft Carriers	34,500	2		0
Light Carriers		0	8,500	1
Heavy Cruisers	56,925	6	26,400	3
Light Cruisers	12,000	2	5,700	1
Destroyers	22,815	14	20,930	11
Submarines		0	11,309	6
Total	126,240	24	134,839	24

BIBLIOGRAPHY

ACTION REPORTS: All U.S. ships in the Guadal-
    canal Campaign; Janac Reports, and individual diaries
    of persons concerned.
*History of the United States Naval Operations in World
    War II*, Vols. IV and V, by Rear Admiral Samuel Eliot
    Morison, USNR, Atlantic-Little, Brown and Company,
    1949 and 1951.
Battle Reports, Vols. II and III, by Captain Walter Karig,
    USNR and Commander Eric Purdon, ISNR, Rinehart
    & Co., 1947.
The Marines' War, by Fletcher Pratt, William Sloan
    Associates, 1948.
The Battle of Savo Island, by Captain Toshikazau Ohmae,
    edited by Roger Pineau, U.S. Naval Institute Proceed-
    ings, December, 1957.
Savo, The Incredible Navy Debacle off Guadalcanal, by
    Richard F. Newcomb, Holt, Rinehart & Winston, New
    York, 1961.
The Army Air Forces in World War II, edited by Wesley
    Frank Craven and James Lea Cate, University of
    Chicago Press, 1953.
The Great Sea War, edited by E. B. Potter and Fleet
    Admiral Chester W. Nimitz, USN, Prentice-Hall, Inc.,
    1960.
The Guadalcanal Campaign, by Major John L. Zimmer-
    man, USMCR, U.S. Marine Corps, Historical Division,
    1949.
Fleet Admiral King, A Naval Record, by Fleet Admiral

Ernest J. King, USN, and Walter Muir Whitehill, W. W. Norton and Company, Inc., 1952.

Military Heritage of America, by Col. R. E. Dupuy, U.S. Army (Ret.) and Col. T. N. Dupuy, U.S. Army, McGraw-Hill Book Co., 1956.

Pacific Battle Line, by Foster Hailey, The Macmillan Co., 1944.

Japanese Destroyer, by Captain Taneichi Hara, with Fred Sarto and Roger Pineau, Ballantine Books, 1961.

The Coastwatchers, by Commander Eric A. Feldt, RAN, Oxford University Press, 1946.

Midway, by Captain Mitsui Fuchida, IJN, and Commander Masatake Okumiya, IJN, United States Naval Institute, 1955.

Pick Out The Biggest, by Frank Morris, Houghton Mifflin Co., 1943.

Mysteries of the Pacific, by Robert de la Croix, John Day Co., 1957.

A Log of the Vincennes, by Johnathan Truman Dorris, The Standard Printing Company, Louisville, Ky., 1947.

Ships in Distress, by J. H. Adams, The Currawan Publishing Co., 1944.

Submarine Operations in World War II, by Theodore Roscoe, U.S. Naval Institute, 1949.

The 100 Best True Stories of World War II, William H. Wise & Co., 1945.

Destroyer Operations in World War II, by Theodore Roscoe, U.S. Naval Institute, 1953.

Guadalcanal Diary, by Richard Tregaskis, Random House, 1943.

The Splendid Little War, by Frank Freidel, Little, Brown, 1958.

The Silent Service, by T. M. Jones and Ion L. Idriess, Angus and Robertson, 1944.

Through the Perilous Night, by Joe James Custer, The Macmillan Company, 1944.

Marine!, by Burke Davis, Little Brown & Co., 1962.

The Battle of Savo, by Stan Smith, MacFadden-Bartell Corp., New York, 1962.

A Military History of the Western World, by Major General J. F. C. Fuller, Funk & Wagnall Co., 1956.